D1201543

CHICAGO PUBLIC LIBRARY
SOCIAL SCIENCES AND HISTORY
400 S. STATE ST. 60605

R00968 69379

MEMORY AND HISTORY

Essays on Recalling and Interpreting Experience

Paul Thompson
Michael H. Frisch
Karen E. Fields
Howard S. Hoffman
Lewis M. Barker
Elizabeth F. Loftus
Marigold Linton
Alice M. Hoffman
Donald A. Ritchie

Edited by Jaclyn Jeffrey
and Glenace Edwall

Lanham • New York • London

INSTITUTE FOR
ORAL HISTORY

Copyright © 1994 by
University Press of America®, Inc.
4720 Boston Way
Lanham, Maryland 20706

3 Henrietta Street
London WC2E 8LU England

All rights reserved
Printed in the United States of America
British Cataloging in Publication Information Available

Co-published by arrangement with the
Institute for Oral History

Michael Frisch's article has appeared previously in the *Journal of American History* 75 (1989): 1130-55 and in *A Shared Authority: Essays on the Craft and Meaning of Oral and Public History* (State University of New York at Buffalo Press, 1991).

Library of Congress Cataloging-in-Publication Data

Memory and history : essays on recalling and interpreting experience / edited by Jaclyn Jeffrey and Glenace Edwall ; [essays by] Paul Thompson... [et al.].
p. cm.
Papers presented at a conference sponsored by the Baylor University Institute for Oral History in 1988.
Includes bibliographical references.
1. Memory—Congresses. 2. Oral history—Congresses. 3. Recollection (Psychology)—Congresses.
I. Jeffrey, Jaclyn. II. Edwall, Glenace Ecklund.
BF371.M448 1994b 153.1'2—dc20 94–1583 CIP

ISBN 0–8191–9460–3 (cloth : alk. paper)
ISBN 0–8191–9508–1 (pbk. : alk. paper)

The paper used in this publication meets the minimum requirements of American National Standard for Information Sciences—Permanence of Paper for Printed Library Materials, ANSI Z39.48–1984.

CHICAGO PUBLIC LIBRARY
SOCIAL SCIENCES AND HISTORY
400 S. STATE ST. 60605

Contents

R00968 69379

FOREWORD

Donald A. Ritchie

Donald A. Ritchie is Associate Historian in the U.S. Senate Historical Office. He is the author of James M. Landis: Dean of the Regulators *and* Press Gallery: Congress and the Washington Correspondents *and is past president of the Oral History Association.*

The sociologist C. Wright Mills once wrote that "The historian represents the organized memory" of society.[1] If so, then the oral historian collects society's otherwise unorganized memories. Oral history is an active process in which interviewers seek out, record, and preserve people's stories and observations. In their quest, oral historians conduct preparatory research so they can coax and guide interviewees, provide a ready supply of forgotten names and dates, give some context and structure to the dialogue through their questions and the order in which they ask them, and challenge any seeming misstatements and contradictions in the testimony. Ultimately, however, interviewers must depend upon the reliability of the interviewees' memories.

The "organized memory" traditionally entrusted to historians reflects how a whole society or its component groups recall and interpret their past. By contrast, oral historians work with individual memories, which can range from sharp to dim. Those historians trained to rely chiefly upon documents often express distrust for memory as a source, dismissing individual memories as self-serving and exaggerated. Oral historians concede that dealing with memory is a risky business, but it is inescapably the interviewer's business.[2] Since the reliability of oral history is bound to the reliability of memory, Baylor University's Memory and History symposium therefore asked the necessary question: What do we really know about the phenomenon of memory?

Previous attempts at interdisciplinary examinations of memory produced little common ground. Psychologists generally studied short-term memory and dealt more with the immediate perception of events. These short-term memory studies gave little assistance to oral historians in explaining the uncanny preciseness with which some interviewees could recall events that took place decades ago, or understanding how interviewees who had reached obvious senility—forgetful even that they

had scheduled the interview—could nevertheless talk authentically abo
events far in the past.[3] The Baylor symposium brought psychologists an
oral historians together to discuss and evaluate both long- and short-ter
memory studies. Although disagreements arose, the exchange wa
remarkably fruitful, demonstrating mutual interests and achievin
considerable consensus.

Both oral historians and psychologists have observed that memory i
largely a matter of personal interpretation. Individuals mentally reconstru
their experiences, so that their memories represent an act of assembly an
of relearning.[4] In this sense, the memories of individuals resemble th
"organized memory" of the historical profession, for, as Mills observed
"Memory, as written history, is enormously malleable. It changes, ofte
quite drastically, from one generation of historians to another."[5] Historian
rewrite history to incorporate new evidence and to fit different interest
and interpretive frameworks. Individuals similarly reshape their memorie
as current events to help them make new sense out of past experiences.

There seems to be a variety of stages through which people's recollec
tions are preserved over time, including perception, retention, rehearsal
reinterpretation, and recall. Interviewees all tell their stories from their ow
subjective points of view. Their individual perceptions vary substantially
since not everyone had a clear view of what happened or a comprehensiv
understanding of what it meant. Generals in the rear may know the broa
sweep of the battle plan, but foot soldiers will have a different view of th
action on the battlefield; those at the center of events can proudly recoun
their own accomplishments, but those on the periphery are often bette
able to make comparisons between the principal actors. Perceptions tha
were originally flawed will produce flawed memories. Distant and routine
actions and second-hand information will be more susceptible to outside
manipulation and distortion. By contrast, direct, dramatic, and emotional
situations tend to produce more lasting and unchanging memories. For
these reasons, oral history projects attempt to collect a wide range of
interviews, to piece the puzzle together from a variety of perspectives.

Not everything perceived is retained. When the television journalist
David Brinkley was writing *Washington Goes to War*, which covered the
years during the Second World War when he first arrived in the capital as a
young broadcaster, he was surprised to find so much in the old newspaper
files that had faded from his memory. "I've always thought I had a good
memory. Now I know I don't," he commented. "Things I knew very well
and in fact stood and watched and interviewed people about, I'd totally
forgotten. That was the startling thing—how much I'd forgotten."[6]

FOREWORD

Information once considered meaningful can become so irrelevant, routine, or insignificant that it is no longer recalled. David Brinkley still concerns himself with today's news and uses his memory of the past to make sense out of current events. But the more distant an occurrence becomes from this week's headlines, the less likely he will think about or retain it. This recalls some sage advice from an old professor: When writing a book an author invariably collects more data than can be used. To cope with the painful task of cutting out material arduously acquired, he recommended putting the excised sections into a folder marked: "For articles I intend to write in the future." Ten years later, the author can take the folder out of the file cabinet and throw it away. By now long forgotten, it will no longer hurt as much to discard.

Rehearsal is another key ingredient in memory retention. Everyone tells stories about past experiences to relive glory days, to celebrate shared experiences, or to make comparisons to the present. Each telling of the story becomes a rehearsal for the next telling, embedding it all the firmer in one's mind. I once used an oral history that Columbia University did with Ferdinand Pecora, a lawyer and judge whose greatest triumph occurred during the early New Deal years when he conducted a highly publicized investigation of Wall Street banking and stock market malpractice. The voluminous transcript of his interview, which took place forty years after the investigation, was remarkable for its detail and precision. When I mentioned this to Pecora's son, he assured me that his father would tell those stories to anyone who would listen, and even on his deathbed he was telling them to the hospital nurses.

Yet, while important for retaining memory, rehearsal can create stumbling blocks for interviewers. Every telling of a story perfects it and moves it further from reality. Events are telescoped, chronology tightened, order rearranged and edited. Rehearsed stories often tend to omit negative events and concentrate on triumphs. Interviewees rarely reconstruct dialogue in which they did not have the last word or achieve the perfect squelch. They have not necessarily forgotten old wounds and mistakes. When questioned, interviewees can recall past defeats, even if they do not always feel comfortable talking about them. But often by the time the oral historian asks the question, the answer will simply be the oft-told story. A well-researched interviewer may spot inaccuracies and gently challenge inconsistencies, but the interviewee may have told the story so often that he or she simply cannot remember it any other way. Under such circumstances, all that an interviewer can do is to give stories and, when the supply is finally exhausted, try to retake control of the interview with questions that will lead down less rehearsed paths.[7]

MEMORY AND HISTORY

Historians are not the only ones who can benefit from hindsigh Sometimes only the passage of time enables people to make sense out c earlier events in their lives. Actions take on new significance depending o their later consequences. Certain people become more important in th story, while the influence of others is downgraded. Like historians, indi viduals reinterpret their historical memories and recast earlier judgment Their later memories may take on a more mature, mellower, or disillusione cast, often depending on the condition of the individual at the time of th interview. Moreover, oral historians by necessity tend to intervie "survivors," those who lived through it, stuck to it, stayed behind, o otherwise succeeded, all factors that shape how and what they remember.

Oral historians have explored the use of artifacts to trigger recall. In a interview with a retired newspaper photographer, I found that ever picture reminded him of a story about that person or event or how he sho the photograph. The photodocumentation provided the clues an structure needed to unlock his memories.[8] Family photo albums newspaper clippings, letters, and other archival documents have all prove helpful tools for unearthing long-"forgotten" information. Som interviewers have even experimented with the sense of smell to unloc memories and get them on tape.

Recognizing that most people do not readily remember names an dates and that the flow of narration can stop short when an interviewe gropes for a name, interviewers attempt to become familiar with the majo players in the interviewee's life and its basic chronology. Providing names and dates also puts interviewees at ease, since some see an oral history as almost a test of their memories, worry that they should review for it, and apologize for any lapses.

Interviewers need to take into account all facets of memory. Are these creditable witnesses? Were they in a position to experience events first-hand, or are they simply passing along second-hand information? What biases might have shaped their original perceptions? Have interviewees forgotten much of their past because it was no longer important to them or because the events were so routine that they were simply not memorable? How differently do interviewees feel now than they did at the time the original events took place? What subsequent incidents might have caused them to rethink and reinterpret their past? How closely does their testimony agree with other documentary evidence from the period, and how do they explain the discrepancies?

During the course of the symposium, I found most appealing the suggestion that memory was less a photograph of the original image than a montage of images and suggestions. Interviewers who have encountered a wide variety of memories will agree that memory may be a montage, but not a hodgepodge, for people frequently remember stories—especially of significant personal incidents—in a reasonably orderly, chronological, and verifiable narrative. The memories of direct participants are far too rich a source for historical researchers to ignore. The message of the Baylor symposium is that interviewers need to become aware of the peculiarities of memory, imaginative in their methods of dealing with it, conscious of its limitations, and open to its abundant treasures.

Notes

1. C. Wright Mills, *The Sociological Imagination* (New York: Oxford University Press, 1959), 144.
2. "Memory has always proven difficult for historians to confront," Michael Frisch noted in his essay, "The Memory of History," in *A Shared Authority: Essays on the Craft and Meaning of Oral and Public History* (Albany: State University of New York Press, 1990), 15-27; see also David Thelen, "Memory and History," *Journal of American History* 75 (March 1989): 1117-29.
3. See John Neuenschwander, "Oral Historians and Long-Term Memory," in David K. Dunaway and Willa K. Baum, eds., *Oral History: An Interdisciplinary Anthology* (Nashville: American Association of State and Local History, 1984), 324-32; and James W. Lomax and Charles T. Morrissey, "The Interview as Inquiry for Psychiatrists and Oral Historians: Convergence and Divergence in Skills and Goals," in *The Public Historian* 11 (Winter 1989): 17-24.
4. See Jean Piaget, *Memory and Intelligence* (New York: Basic Books, 1973); and Edmund Blair Bolles, *Remembering and Forgetting: Inquiries into the Nature of Memory* (New York: Walker and Company, 1988).
5. Mills, *The Sociological Imagination*, 144-45.
6. David Brinkley, *Washington Goes to War* (New York: Alfred Knopf, 1988); and "The Conversation: Arthur Schlesinger, Jr. Interviews David Brinkley," *Washington Post Magazine*, 10 April 1988, 29.
7. An interesting case study can be found in Mary Elizabeth Aubé, "Oral History and the Remembered World: Cultural Determinants from French Canada," *International Journal of Oral History* 10 (February 1989): 31-49.
8. George Tames, Washington Photographer for the *New York Times*, 1945-1985, Oral History Interviews, January 13 to May 16, 1988, Senate Historical Office, Washington, D.C.

INTRODUCTION

The title of this book, *Memory and History*, reflects the binary nature of its contents: the viewpoints of scholars from two fields, cognitive psychology and oral history, looking at the ways in which human experience is recalled and interpreted. The two fields carry with them certain approaches to research that have not always been perceived as compatible. Oral history was born out of fieldwork, and its nature is experiential, contextual, and expressive. Cognitive psychology has traditionally operated in the laboratory and is therefore experimental, narrower in scope, and more highly defined in structure. The goal of this collection of papers is to use this interplay between natural setting and experimental investigation to deepen our understanding of human memory and its processes.

The papers collected in this volume were first presented in 1988 at a conference sponsored by the Baylor University Institute for Oral History. As far as we know, that gathering of oral historians and cognitive psychologists to exchange ideas on memory was the first of its kind. It seemed highly desirable to bring all of the papers together in one volume for, if each were published only in its own discipline, as most articles are, the results would be scattered to disparate scholarly audiences. The conference was an exercise in interdisciplinary thinking, and so it is with this book of proceedings.

In the first paper, historian Paul Thompson sets the theme of dualism by noting the tension between the two ideas, memory and history. As an advocate of the kind of open-ended research that forges connections between studies, he demonstrates its use by bridging the gap between individual and collective memory, and between historical fact and cultural myth. Psychologist Elizabeth F. Loftus provides the scientific undergirding for assessing the reliability of memory by explaining her research on short-term individual memory. Historian Michael H. Frisch then examines collective memory in United States culture and how, contrary to popular thought, it is molded according to very consistent traditional norms. Oral historians and others seeking advice on how best to tap into individual memory will be particularly interested in psychologist Marigold Linton's presentation on long-term memory. Historian Karen E. Fields provides another bridge to connect individual with collective memory as she intertwines individual, family, and group memory. The wife-husband team, historian Alice M. Hoffman and psychologist Howard S. Hoffman, conclude the main body of the volume discussing their project on the reliability of memory in which they compared documented fact with individual long-term memory.

In order to extend the scope of the papers and place them into broader contexts, each major paper is followed by a brief commentary from a scholar in another field—history, psychology, speech communication, or cultural geography. The two dialogue sections deserve special attention. Each presents an edited transcription of a panel discussion among the scholars, a truly interdisciplinary, collaborative effort. Finally, in an effort to balance the "tension" between psychology and history, we asked historian Donald A. Ritchie and psychologist Lewis M. Barker to introduce and conclude the book, respectively. And, like two very solid bookends, they buttress the presentations between them, extending and supporting the contents.

While both oral historians and cognitive psychologists have focused their attention primarily upon individual memory, in this volume their explorations occasionally lead to examining *collective* memory as well. Individual memory as it is discussed here refers for the most part to studies conducted with the English or with "mainstream" Americans. This limitation clearly restricts the application of much of what is presented here, even within our own country, but at the same time it suggests a fertile area for future memory research. For example, we know that people in Western cultures tend to perceive experiences in linear ways, as a series of causes and effects, which surely shapes memory in specific ways. How then is memory shaped in societies where individuals perceive events more synchronically? How do theories of memory hold up across generations, across regions, or across cultures? Many more collaborations are needed here, and many are currently in progress. It is interesting to see how collective memory imposed itself upon this volume of what was originally intended to be a study of individual memory alone. Perhaps it reflects a growing realization in American scholarship that even in memory the individual and the community are more closely intertwined than traditionally perceived. If our cultural heritage is the mold that we are given to pour our memories into, then memory studies must necessarily include cultural studies.

Recent research on the human brain suggests that interdisciplinary research is more critical and relevant than ever before. For example, current studies in Japan and in the United States suggest that language and sexual orientation not only order our world view for us but may actually affect the ways in which brain cells develop. If culture or experience is found to help determine brain physiology, then the need for interdisciplinary studies among the humanities, the social sciences, and the biological sciences will be not merely beneficial but *necessary* to the continued expansion of our knowledge base. One of the goals of this collection is to foster interest in an interdisciplinary approach to the study of memory and history. We hope that it is the beginning of many more such efforts as we all go about our studies of human experience in its multitude of forms.

Special appreciation is extended to Baylor University for its generous support for this project. At the Institute for Oral History, Thomas L. Charlton, David Stricklin, Lois Myers, and Rebecca Sharpless provided collegial support and encouragement, while Janice O'Bryant, Peggy Kinard, Norfleete Day, and and Cindy Wranowsky lent their skills and expertise to aid in its production. Other individuals in the Baylor community contributed to the Memory and History symposium, and hence to this publication, and so we extend our gratitude to President Herbert H. Reynolds for his longtime interest in and encouragement of oral history research; the Department of Psychology and its chair, Helen E. Benedict; John S. Belew, Executive Vice President for Academic Affairs; Bruce C. Cresson, Dean of the University School; and Rufus B. Spain, Professor of History.

BELIEVE IT OR NOT: RETHINKING THE HISTORICAL INTERPRETATION OF MEMORY

Paul Thompson

In this paper Paul Thompson, British social historian and leading scholar in the international oral history movement, examines the relation of human memory to the social and cultural milieu in which it exists. Thompson is a research professor in social history at the University of Essex and director of the National Life Story Collection at the National Sound Archive in London. He is a longtime advocate of interdisciplinary research who uses that approach here to investigate the ways in which memory and oral tradition have been studied. He explains how, as a young historian in the 1960s, he first worked with social scientists using oral history research, confident in the belief that if the questions were carefully framed the answers would reveal historical truth. In his classic study of oral history, The Voice of the Past *(1978 and 1988), Thompson expanded his approach to consider the conceptualization of experience as a factor in the reliability of memory. Here he concludes that the interrelatedness of human memory to its context demands that we study memory in a similarly interrelated way. In* The Myths We Live By *(1990), he joined other scholars in examining truth and myth in individual and collective memory.*

"Believe it or not": The essential tension found in that phrase reflects the controversy within the title of this symposium, Memory and History, because, for many people, there is a tension between those two ideas. On the one hand, we have the idea of History—History with a capital *H*; History, the permanent record; History, the proud, bound volumes on the library shelves, the Statue of Liberty, the state and religious ceremonial. We are all familiar with History in the university, in the style of the buildings, and even in some of the comments in their publications. For instance, in Baylor University's brochure I find the suggestion that a teacher affects eternity: "With our long tradition of fine teaching at Baylor, we keep students and eternity in mind." That is the claim of public History with a capital *H*.

Against that bold claim we have to set what we all know so personally as so much less firm: memory, and with it our feeling that our memory—

personal memory, private memory—isn't quite adequate. There are things that we are not sure we should tell or could tell, and yet at the same time memory reaches back into our own childhood beginnings and, in spite of being blurred and patchy and a bit confused, is central to our own sense of who we are. There will be some of us who want to hold very strongly to that contrast between concretely documented history and the story of personal experience, who want to emphasize the distinction between history which is firmly constructed, reliable, and permanent, and the imperfections of personal memory, and who will want to see memory more as a door to our own consciousness than as matter for reconstructing the past.

Ronald Fraser's recent autobiography, *In Search of a Past*,[1] which started from his own explorations into the setting of his childhood, addresses that view of history and memory. Fraser grew up as a wealthy, isolated, rather snooty little boy in the countryside outside London, brought up largely by his nanny and other servants, including a gardener, rather than by his aloof mother and father. In middle age he returned to interview the survivors from that household and tried to reconstruct a picture, through oral history, of the context of his own childhood. In that marvelous and very brave book, Fraser interweaves these recollections between himself and his own psychoanalyst with two other levels of memory. One is the disintegrated memory of his father, whose mind is now mere fragments of past sense. The other comes through a dialogue, and one of the most striking things about that dialogue is how the psychoanalyst is simply not interested in Fraser's memory as a source of history for a *real* past. He keeps saying, "It doesn't matter what really happened. All that matters is what you feel about it. Let's have some more of your feelings." And for a historian, that is a completely different way of looking at memory.

There are others, and I would hope there are many of us, who would not want to pose such a stark dichotomy between memory and history but would rather see in both aspects the same thing, perhaps with a different emphasis. On the one hand, some would recognize personal memory as the thread of every individual's life history, central to each person's understanding of themselves and their own sense of both history and self. On the other hand, they would perceive public history, for all its pretensions, to be no more and no less than the accepted modern version of old-fashioned, traditional, collective memory—the functional equivalent to the traditions passed down orally in nonliterate societies but now transmitted in a much more complicated way, through buildings and scholarships and media and ceremonial. Nevertheless, in a larger sense the public history of our own time remains, despite the skeptical efforts of scholarly history, our own collective memory. So you really have two aspects of memory and two aspects of history, personal and collective.

Now, to talk that way is to talk very differently from the way in which we oral historians used to talk ten years ago. I should like to indicate some of the implications of this new view by discussing the changes I have been making in revising my book, *The Voice of the Past*, which has just come out in a new edition.[2] It was first published in 1978; I have come back to it after an interval of a decade, and I am struck by how very differently I see things now. Let me go back to the spirit in which it was written. I had been working for about ten years as an historian before I stumbled into oral history at the end of the 1960s. I was then a social historian working alongside social scientists. My first big oral history research project was a representative study of over four hundred old men and women in Britain, focusing on family life and work life in the years before 1918—a study which I published as *The Edwardians*.[3] I began that study very much in the spirit of the sociologists who were then my colleagues, and I saw the problems of oral history as they saw them at that time; that is to say, that people could be asked questions and then somehow speak a kind of truth which could be taken for granted. They did not think too much about it. They were, however, concerned about rather specific sources of bias. They laid great emphasis on who you interviewed—how you chose your sample—and that is something I addressed in *The Voice of the Past*. They were also concerned about the techniques of interviewing, how you framed questions. They had an underlying assumption that if you purged an interview of what was called bias, you would reach an uncontaminated version of the truth which simply had to be tapped from within the informant. They saw the main problem as being whether that information within the informant was distorted or contaminated by the passage of time, by remembering, or by reevaluating earlier memories. They were not, in other words, concerned with what we now see as the essential mental processes of thinking about experience, of conceiving it in order to express it.

I think that oral historians, in general, were working very much in that spirit at the time. That explains why we had such an enthusiasm for the idea that through oral history you could somehow reach immediately to the past: that if you knew how to interview, you could tap a real past which had been hidden from history simply because people had not carried out interviews. It seemed unproblematic; you just had to start work, and the evidence came. Now, I would still maintain that until you have started interviewing, you really have no idea of the richness of what people have to tell you. For me, the fundamental motivational force for doing oral history work is still the wish to hear what people have to say and the belief in the value of their testimony. But there is no doubt at all that we have moved a long way from that early and rather naive enthusiasm.

In that earlier phase, the most serious problem facing us seemed to be to demonstrate that oral evidence did have a real reliability. So that is a central part of the argument in *The Voice of the Past*. In writing it, I examined many of the classic works on memory which had been published up to that time, and through that, I changed my mind to a certain extent. I came to see that the crucial process to understand was the conceptualization of experience, which took place fairly quickly after an event and provided the form in which the experience would be remembered and could be recalled later. I combined that insight, which I think is fundamental and remains, with a good deal of work on the speed at which people forgot things. The model I held then was that there was a memory store, and that various things, including aging, impinged its effectiveness. There might also be factors which release memory, such as lack of inhibition or the life review process among older people, but there was a basic memory store, and it was either depleted or its contents could be released more easily through these external factors. In that belief, and indeed in the whole approach, there was a very positivistic feeling to the argument. Now, that might be seen as the phrase, "believe it," that the objective of oral historians up to that point was to demonstrate that you could believe it. I think that, to a large extent, we did win that argument. We convinced many skeptical historians that there was sufficient in memory that was reliable; there were dangers and problems and so on, but there was sufficient that was reliable for oral history to be a respectable form of evidence.

But at the point when I was writing, the oral history world was essentially Anglo-Saxon, an American and English one. We had only just begun to make contact with the European oral history movement, which, unknown to me at that time, was already beginning to develop. Over the last decade, there has been a very rapid change in approaches to oral history, partly thanks to the opening up of those influences beyond the classic, positivistic, empirical Anglo-Saxon tradition of scholarship. Those new influences have come to us in different ways. I would want to mention in particular the role which was played by Ronald J. Grele as the first editor of the *International Journal of Oral History*, both in introducing some of the ideas from Europe to a wider audience and also in his special propagation of social scientific insights—particularly from anthropology—into the nature of the interview process, such as the two-way relationship between the interviewer and the informant and the social context of the interview in the field.

A second major source has been the group of sociologists working with life stories. In particular, I would mention Daniel Bertaux, a French sociologist. His special interest has been in using life-story evidence to understand social mobility—to understand how people move through the social system, why they make their choices—and therefore, on the one hand to use that evidence again in a positivistic way. But right from the beginning he and his group have been extremely interested in the way in which that life experience was differently remembered by different social groups. One of his first works with Isabelle Bertaux-Wiame[4] was about French bakers, both master bakers and employees, all of whom had started as bakers' apprentices. The Bertauxes found in their interviews with the bakers that the facts they told about their youth were broadly the same, but the way in which they presented the story was quite different. For those who remained workers throughout their lives, their stories of apprenticeship were of hardship, long hours, working right through the night, often very rough treatment by the master, small wages, and so on. For those who remained workers, that was a story of exploitation which continued right through their lives. But for those who became masters, those years of apprenticeship were seen as a very useful, very valuable educative experience, a kind of gateway, a hardening process through which they had beneficially passed, so that their whole interpretation was presented in a different way. This insight from the bakers' interviews is characteristic of the more subtle way in which Bertaux and the life-story sociologists approached their evidence right from the beginning.

More broadly, there were also two notable interests among both French and Italian historians which influenced the oral history movement. The first was in collective memory, the processes by which European communities developed their own historical traditions, shaped them, and used them. The second was in what they called "subjectivity," a word which does not really have a proper equivalent in English, because *subjectivity* combines the sense of consciousness with the sense of self, self-identity; it brings together those ideas. It always creates a difficulty when it is used in English, because to us it suggests a direct contrast with objectivity, something which is by its nature somehow distorted—biased. In French or Italian it has a broader, more positive meaning, and in this sense has been a major theme of the thinking of oral historians from these countries. Closely connected with subjectivity has been an interest in not just the conscious self but also the unconscious self.

Now, to my mind these new influences have created great new opportunities for oral historians everywhere. But I think that they have also created dangers. I want to highlight three of the most important areas in which those influences are now operating on us.

The first concerns the processes of what may be variously called oral tradition or collective memory or collective myth—how you name these things depends on where you are. If you are in a nonliterate society, you are more likely to be talking about oral tradition. If you are in a literate society, you are more likely to be talking about collective memory. But the processes are very similar.

There has been here, first of all, a longstanding debate about whether oral tradition has any intrinsic value for historians at all in the sense of conveying messages about the reality of the past. You can see this very well in the changes which have occurred between the first and the last editions (1961 and 1985) of Jan Vansina's book, *Oral Tradition*.[5] Vansina was a Belgian historian who started working in the Congo and there discovered the value of oral tradition for political history in a society bereft of written record. He set out in his book to show that oral evidence could be collected, tested, and evaluated. He saw oral traditions as documents from the past which had been handed down orally rather than in written form over time. Vansina's objective was closely parallel to our own aims in oral history. Both of us were looking for the purest version which memory could offer us of the past.

Since then Vansina has been conducting a running battle, particularly with anthropologists of the functionalist school, who have argued, like their founder Malinowski, that what people say about the past simply reflects their needs at the present. According to this purely functionalist view of the transmission of history, if people continue to hand down a tradition, they claim it as their own because they need it now. Thus the genealogy of a royal dynasty exists to prove that the present incumbent has the right to the throne, while family traditions are handed down less publicly to maintain that the family has a right to the land on which they are settled. And if the rights that they need to claim are changed, then the oral tradition will change.

Now, Vansina has resolutely continued to reject that absolutely defeatist functionalist position. And in the recent second edition of his book, retitled *Oral Tradition as History*, he argues very strongly to the contrary, concluding,

> Yes, oral traditions are documents *of the present*, because they are told in the present. Yet they also embody a message from the past, so they are expressions *of the past* at the same time. They are the representation of the past in the present. One cannot deny either the present or the past in them. To attribute their whole content to the evanescent present as some sociologists do, is to mutilate tradition; it is reductionistic. To ignore the impact of the present as some historians have done, is equally reductionistic. Traditions must always be understood as reflecting both past and present in a single breath.[6]

If you took the extreme view, it would be quite impossible to explain how anyone could have invented all the rich material in tradition just to be useful in the present. It simply is beyond social imagination to create all that tradition on the spot as needed. At the very least, either from reality or imaginatively it must incorporate a part of the past. And again, if you took a purely functionalist view, you could not explain the many major cultural continuities which, as we all know, often last long beyond their apparent functional need and basis.

However, Vansina has shifted very considerably in taking that new and more balanced view. He has increasingly looked at reasons for forgetting, as well as the mechanics of handing down traditions. This has brought him closer to the work which has been carried out particularly by French and Italian oral historians on collective memory, collective myth, and tradition in Western societies. The sense of self-protectiveness in the maintenance of traditions is undoubtedly valid and needs to be understood. Vansina found it in East Africa and it can be found equally in Europe. There are very telling examples, such as Jerome Mintz's *The Anarchists of Casa Viejas* (1982),[7] from Spain in the civil war period, of how the anarchists totally concealed the story of their own history right through the ensuing Franco years. They did not forget it, but they simply would not tell it. It was only much more recently that those stories could be told. That is an extreme instance of a form of pressure that will always help shape what is recalled.

By contrast with Vansina and other Africanists, Western oral historians have only recently begun to look at a process which needs much more attention, the process of historical transmission: of how we learn history, teach it, hand it down. There are very interesting examples of how this is done among French Protestants, a minority group who over the centuries has suffered considerable persecution and whose history is, therefore, very special to their identity as a community. Not only do families take their children to the cemeteries—as they do in much of France—but they also take them up into the mountains and show them the rocks where their ancestors hid from the French army, the circles of beech trees where groups of Protestants would gather together for outdoor ceremonies and hold their religious services. Their way of remembering their own past has not only affected their view of the history of Protestantism but also of more recent history. When they tell their own story in interviews, these French Protestants speak of the history of World War II and their own help for the Jews threatened by Nazi persecution, many of whom they hid and rescued, very much in terms of their own earlier history, and they tell it in the same way. They have a very distinctive way of talking about the war years, quite different from what is typical in France.

We could do very much more worthwhile work of this kind, for not nearly enough is known about how history is handed down in Anglo-Saxon societies. The taking of children to the cemetery is something that happened certainly in the past in England but is now abandoned. Telling family history undoubtedly goes on, but we have scarcely studied how it happens. And to my knowledge, the only area where we have much evidence of that in print is with upper-class English families, among whom the handing down of family history is not only through telling about traditions of the past but also through its physical monuments, through the family house which plays such a very central part in their family culture. In English upper-class autobiography the importance of the house has a unique place, quite different from autobiography in other classes. I have found autobiographies which open not typically with descriptions of parents and grandparents but with descriptions of a series of houses; Chapter 1 is this house, and Chapter 2 is that house. The people in the family come in as almost incidental occupants, because for them the family tradition is literally embodied in brick or stone. We need to know much more about how both family history and wider historical concepts, facts, and traditions are transmitted at different social levels.

An example of how fruitful this can be comes in the work of Alessandro Portelli on the Italian steel town of Terni,[8] where through interviewing many older steelworkers, he has been able to show the ways in which they have created a coherent collective myth out of the past. When talking about their lives, these steelworkers constantly move incidents from one context to another. The story of the killing of a worker, for instance, is moved from an anti-NATO demonstration to mass protests against redundancies among the steelworkers, because one provides a more meaningful context than the other. And more than that, Portelli shows that people actually invent history. They tell stories about things that they did on particular occasions which never happened at all, and they also tell stories about what they might have done—how history might have been different if they had done something else. Portelli makes a very persuasive argument for a totally different way of looking at memory: memory as a form of consciousness, that is in itself historical fact. Portelli points out that "the death of Luigi Trastulli [the worker who was shot] would not mean so much to the historian if it were remembered 'right.' . . . What makes it meaningful . . . is the way it operates in people's memories." Thirty, forty years later, in the *longue durée* of memory, Trastulli's death still echoes in popular imagination. "The fact that people remember, the way they remember (and forget) are themselves the stuff of which history is made." Furthermore, he claims, "Subjectivity is as much the business of history as are the more visible 'facts.' What informants believe is indeed a historical *fact* (that is, the fact that they believe it), as much as what really happened."[9]

Portelli goes on even more strongly to say, "Oral sources are credible but with a *different* credibility. The importance of oral testimony may lie not in its adherence to fact, but rather in its departure from it, as imagination, symbolism, and desire emerge. Therefore, there are no 'false' oral sources."[10] Now, that is the extreme "don't believe it" position: don't believe it, but make use of it. Malinowski's functionalism is accepted and then turned on its head. I think we must question that position very strongly. It is very intriguing and very persuasive, but I would not want to go the whole way with it. It is a rewarding but also a very dangerous position.

The second major new approach has been to draw on literary forms of analysis. These are again promising but at the same time dangerous—and in different ways. Interesting literary work about storytelling and the structural, grammatical, and stylistic forms in which stories are told, has been conducted by, for instance, William Labov in America. Parallel with this has been the hermeneutic school, with its focus on the interaction between the interviewer and the informant. Both perspectives can tell us a lot about the kinds of material we are dealing with. But I want to warn against the risk in their leading to a merely self-stimulating circular process, through which we become more and more involved with the linguistic or interactional structure of the memory we are examining, and less and less concerned about the message which is actually there in the memory. That is, I believe, a serious danger.

With this in mind I would want to point towards another area of literary evidence, which is again very promising, but still less developed. That is the genre approach: the method of looking at the literary motifs and forms which have been used in spoken testimony to try to sort out what is conventional in the telling of a particular life story, what those conventions imply, and also what is personal and particular. Many of the recollections we record include stories which are partly or wholly old fables, old traditions, incorporated into the individual life story, motifs which are taken from outside. Also, the whole form may be shaped by one genre or another. Luisa Passerini has suggested that many Turinese Communist militants use a form of life story which is very close to earlier stories of the saints, almost a form of hagiography: They speak of "my confession," and they often have a conversion experience as saints used to have. Because they tell their story in that particular form, what they have to say is in part shaped by its expectations.

There is no doubt that we could learn much more through understanding those forms. We also need to compare the forms of oral testimony with those of other forms of autobiography. There has been some work of this kind by Philippe Lejeune in France, but it has been too rarely followed. One example is in work by Stefan Bohman, who has looked at a set of Swedish autobiographies by the same authors who had also recorded oral testimonies and demonstrated how people did write and speak about their pasts in very different ways. His findings were encouraging for us in oral history, for they showed that the written autobiographies tended to be much more formalized and much less immediate, while in the spoken testimony there was a much higher proportion of direct feeling and real particular evidence which could have only come from direct experience. Much more work is needed in this direction.

Then the third and major new approach is to focus on subjectivity and the unconscious. This has been developed particularly by French and Italian scholars. I would draw your attention here to two aspects of it. One is the influence of Jacques Lacan in France—the idea that language is embedded in people's early consciousness, that in fact it shapes their early consciousness, so that, for instance, being a man and being a woman is a part of one's sense of self developed through the presence of gender in language. This influence lies behind Isabelle Bertaux-Wiame's observation that in her interviews men and women told their stories in very different ways. The men tended to speak with the active "I," to put themselves always at the center of the story, not just in content but grammatically as well; while the women tended to talk about "we" or "one" and to see themselves as more passive, as part of a group. A sensitivity of this kind to our material is very important. And you can carry the observation of the words that people use much farther than that. You can use them to distinguish many subtly different levels of ideology—religious or political beliefs, attitudes to the material world, and so on. Such a sensitivity is promising and needs to be developed.

A rather different path towards the subconscious is offered through psychoanalysis, which has been particularly pursued by Luisa Passerini from Italy. First of all, her interest in psychoanalysis led her to a concern, then rare among oral historians, with the meaning of forgetting, with the significance of what was not said. She found that in memories of the interwar years in Turin there were often long blanks, stretches of memory missing, which she suggested reflected the suffering that people had undergone during the fascist era, past wounds evidenced in present repression. In drawing attention to how trauma can affect memory, she offered a very valuable insight and one which can quickly be applied to many other situations. But she has pushed beyond that to an interest in the unconscious and how it can be positively revealed in memory.

Nevertheless, in dialogue between oral history and psychoanalysis, it is not so much what has been done so far which has been fascinating people, as what might be done. Here I want to sound another warning note. Psychoanalysis is very beguiling because it interests us all: It suggests to us that there is something deep within us which somebody could reveal. There is a temptation for oral historians to try to take on some of the power which psychoanalysts wield, the power to listen and, through listening and drawing out these deep inner secrets, to heal people, to ease intense suffering. There is something very attractive in that great power. And because nobody quite understands how they do it, there is a feeling that they have a certain kind of magical potency to interpret the past which we also ought to have. If only we had it, we would be discovering quite different things.

I believe that is a false way of looking at things. It is undoubtedly true that we can learn a lot from psychoanalysis, and also from many other forms of therapy which help to release memory, for the forms of therapy used by groups or in family therapy can be just as powerful as psychoanalysis in releasing memory. We need to know a lot more about them and whether we can usefully borrow from them. But the idea that we will reach a quite different kind of past is not, I think, true. We can learn about what Freud called *dream work*: how the unconscious turns memory around, reverses it, substitutes one thing for another, puts unlikely things together, turns it upside down. We can connect that with the kind of symbolism that we find in collective memory, in public memory, and in ritual, where you also find strange connections made, reversals, things presented upside down. But the elements in all this are always the same kind of things which we find in daily life. They may be in different places, but they are not different in kind. Historical work has shown that even the dreams of schizophrenics reflect the social reality of their times. In the nineteenth century schizophrenics dreamt typically about religion—the obsession of the nineteenth century. And now, today, they dream about sex. If there is an eternal unconscious hidden in the human mind, it can hardly have changed in that particular way. So don't get carried away. Don't think that if you could get your informant to lie back on the couch and to free-associate, you would find a door into a past completely different from anything you ever heard before.

Through all these new approaches we need to keep always in mind our ultimate objective, which is to use personal memory—the unique power of personal memory—to interpret change over time. Over the last ten years we have been coming a long way in doing just that. We need to keep at the forefront the *connecting* value of oral history and oral testimony. That to me seems to be its unique quality; oral history is a connecting value which moves in all sorts of different directions. It connects the old and the young, the academic world and the world outside, but more specifically it allows us to make connections in the interpretation of history; for example, between different places, or different spheres, or different phases of life. That is a unique power of oral history. We can look at migration, for instance, in the work like that of Peter Friedlander or Tamara Hareven or Jerry White—fascinating books which follow migrants from one social context to another, from one continent to another, and also between the different spheres of life, work, family, leisure, and so on. It is this last point, the breaking down between spheres of life, with which I want to conclude, because I think there we can bring together in particularly interesting ways the nature of memory, and how it is handed down, with the nature of social and family change. I see a tremendous new opportunity opening up for us which I would want to be part of our ambitions for the next ten years.

I have come to see this myself through my own recent work on the change in the family in Britain. We have interviewed a sample of a hundred families, and our aim has been to interview three generations in each family. Through this we have come to see the significance not only in patterns of change in family ways of behaving—which can be looked at in a positivist, objective way—but also in the importance of family myths, indeed in the power of family traditions and memory. I know of one family, for example, in which a member of the family was shot for cowardice in the eighteenth century. He is quite a famous figure in British history, Admiral Byng, who was shot for the loss of the isle of Minorca in the Mediterranean in the mid-eighteenth century. Two hundred years later cowardice remains an obsessive issue for men in that family, even to the point of breakdown. It has haunted their dreams, and it has driven some of them to almost foolhardy courage on the frontiers of the Empire. That is perhaps a negative instance of the tradition. But we found how family myth, family memories can have a positive dynamic too. Through looking at those myths and realities, both remembered, together with the dynamic effect they have on the changing life of a family, we have begun to combine the more conventional oral history approach, with which I started, with the approach of family therapy, with its different ways of interpreting people's accounts of their lives. There are problems in transferring techniques from one objective to another which we still have to solve. Put simply, we cannot expect families to spill out their memories to us as they do to a therapist, because we cannot offer them the same help. Nevertheless, this bringing together of new insights and new techniques from those concerned above all with coming to terms with memory subjectively, with making people whole, and those who want to use memory as a portal to history, to know what really happened, to my mind offers our best hope for the next ten years and for this gathering of papers. Returning to my original question, "Believe it or not?," my answer is that we need *both* to believe and to doubt, to make use of what we can believe and also of what we must doubt, and to bring the two together in a new interpretation which fuses both memory and history.

Notes

1. Ronald Fraser, *In Search of a Past: The Manor House, Amnersfield, 1933-1945* (London: Verso, 1984).

2. Paul Thompson, *The Voice of the Past: Oral History* (New York: Oxford University Press, 1988).
3. Paul Thompson, *The Edwardians: The Remaking of British Society* (Bloomington: Indiana University Press, 1975).
4. Isabelle Bertaux-Wiame, "The Life History Approach to the Study of Internal Migration: How Women and Men Came to Paris Between the Wars," in *Our Common History: The Transformation of Europe*, ed. Paul Thompson (London: Pluto Press, 1982), 194.
5. Jan Vansina, *Oral Tradition: A Study in Historical Methodology*, trans. H. M. Wright (London: Routledge & Paul, 1961).
6. Jan Vansina, *Oral Tradition as History* (Madison: University of Wisconsin Press, 1985), xii.
7. Jerome Mintz, *The Anarchists of Casa Viejas* (Chicago: University of Chicago Press, 1982).
8. Alessandro Portelli, *The Death of Luigi Trastulli and Other Stories: Form and Meaning in Oral History* (Albany: State University of New York Press, 1991).
9. Alessandro Portelli, "'The Time of My Life': Functions of Time in Oral History," *International Journal of Oral History* 2, no. 3 (November 1981): 175; Portelli, *The Death of Luigi Trastulli,* 50.
10. Portelli, *The Death of Luigi Trastulli,* 51.
11. Luisa Passerini, *Fascism in Popular Memory: The Cultural Experience of the Turin Working Class*, trans. Robert Lumley and Jude Bloomfield (Cambridge: Cambridge University Press, 1984).
12. Bertaux-Wiame, "The Life History Approach to the Study of Internal Migration," 193.

COMMENT

__Glenace E. Edwall__ is a psychological clinician and a professor of psychology at the University of Minnesota. Long concerned with the processes of memory, here she explores Thompson's ideas about the reliability of memory and the process of oral history in light of her experience as a clinical psychologist.

The oral historian (humanities researcher) and the psychological clinician face several common dilemmas, and Paul Thompson has given us much useful guidance. I especially appreciate his portrayal of individual memory embedded in social context, which both helps to shape it and is also served by it; his sensitivity to both the cognitive-structural components of memory and also the emotional; and his delineation of consistent forms of difference in life experience which many of us as psychologists are only beginning to recognize as our ethical and epistemological responsibility to understand, viz., gender, class, and race. He has raised a number of issues which concern and inform a variety of disciplines.

Five issues raised by Thompson arise in the meeting, speaking, and interpretation of encounters between clinicians and their clients, paralleled to those of oral historians and informants. I had first intended to call these paradoxes, but that seems a bit too grandiose. Perhaps more properly, they are simply tensions with which we live, hopefully more easily for having articulated them.

First is the issue of the nature of the question posed and the type of memory it is likely—and intended—to elicit. As Thompson quite rightly notes, general questioning will encourage the recitation of collective myths and impressions (or lead only to silence), while detailed questions can draw out particular facts and accounts of everyday life. We know this in a number of areas; in my clinical training with Lenore Walker, for example, I saw graphically the different responses likely produced to the question "What is your married life like?" versus "What happened in the battering?" versus "What was the first experience of being beaten like?" Detailed questions are not only tags for memory retrieval, but also normalize experiences and make for a safe environment to retrieve emotionally painful material. But certainly we have also been educated by a number of researchers, from Loftus to Kintsch, Bransford, and others, that the form of the question can elicit both more veridical material and also more material which corresponds to the implications and connotations of the question. We thus often walk the very delicate line of attempting to provide through questions enough structure to aid retrieval without unduly biasing it, a mean feat indeed.

Secondly, Paul Thompson reminds us that silence and even "lies" are interpretable data, surely an important part of the armamentarium of the clinical psychologist. He also reminds us, however, that it requires a knowledge on the part of the hearer which can generate expectations, usually in the form of some sort of theory, in order to notice even these silences and lies, let alone interpret them. The problem here is immediately obvious: That which allows us to hear also allows us to distort, often in the provision of default values derived from theory to cover the silence and explain the lies. It was interesting to me that Thompson spoke of missing referents to sexuality and sexual behavior in several cases. One could ask, however, to what extent the understanding of such data as missing and certainly the interpretation of its absence as due to repressive shame is itself a Freudian-inspired construction which may not fit—at least in exact detail—what the informants in fact experienced. The publication of the Freud-Fliess correspondence[1] has shown us even more dramatically the extent to which the most brilliant of clinicians may begin to see theoretical constructions so clearly that even obvious aspects of reality must yield to them. My point is not to rail against either Freudian theory in particular nor formal/informal theories in general, since they are necessary to seeing, but to remember the two-edged nature of their contribution.

This leads to a third and related point: the more general contribution of the knower, in this case the interviewer/clinician, to the material being remembered and interpreted. This was implicit in Thompson's discussion of the various uses and interpretations of oral data, but I would like to be more explicit for psychological data: we may hear best—in some sense, even most objectively—when we share a frame of reference with a client which allows us to enter her subjectively. I choose to say "her" purposefully, because I know that I understand my female clients differently and better than male, more for this reason (intersubjectivity) than because of explicit politics. In this shared form, however, I also immediately run more risk of overwhelming the particular and unique voice which it is my task to hear, because of my greater ease of appropriating it into or as my own. Quite paradoxically, I may have to work hardest to create distance in those relationships of greatest commonality so that the unique can be differentiated from the common, the individual from the social.

Fourth, Thompson reminded me of the enormous power of telling and the emotion it often releases. Further increasing this power, social psychology has shown us that if you would like to buy someone's loyalty, don't do him a favor; have him do you one. We are either explicitly (oral historians) or perhaps more subtly (clinicians) in the business of asking people to do us the favor of telling us their stories to serve our ends; when they do so and in the process also experience the catharsis associated with telling, they have given us great power. Again, though, this is only one side: the power to give is also the power to take away or to withhold. The other side of the power of telling which Thompson describes is the power not to tell, to keep one's secrets. Just as the interviewer needs to be aware of the emotional energy which may accompany telling, she must also be respectful of the emotion invested in not telling. Perhaps this is simply a long way of saying that interviewers in both disciplines may also need sensitivity to the resistance and even hostility their questions may engender, and to see this as a springing from the same root as the powerful relief and ego enhancement Thompson describes.

Last, Thompson reminds us that memory contains both facts and myths, and that both are meaning structures of consequence to the individual and to the listener. I would heartily agree, but I again think there is an implicit point in Thompson's discussion which also informs much clinical work:

both fact and myth have meaning, but they may not be equivalen meanings. In the wake of Jeffrey Masson's book, which I alluded t above, a rather standard response from the "normal science" viewpoin was that it really didn't matter whether a given adult woman's report of a incestuous relationship as a child was "really" a memory or "really" fantasy, since what was of actual consequence was the meaning given t the memorial structure by the woman herself. Perhaps this is a moo distinction for some memorial material, but psychiatrists Denise Gelinas[2] and Elaine Carmen[3] and others agree that for many incest victims, it is not The accuracy or fallibility of one's perceptions, and thus one's status as knower and as a self are very much at stake in the distinction, as witnesse by the power in uncovering long-hidden (buried) truths of one's experience. I have no particular wisdom on ascertaining the distinction i problematic cases, but I would encourage us not to abandon the potentia meaning in the distinction because of our epistemological or theoretica difficulties. I love the "Saturday Night Live" line, "Hear me now and believe me later." Sometimes, that may be all we can do.

Notes

1. Jeffrey M. Masson, ed., *The Complete Letters of Sigmund Freud to Wilhelm Fliess, 1887-1904* (Cambridge, Mass.: Harvard University Press, 1985).
2. Denise Gelinas, "The Persisting Negative Effects of Incest," *Psychiatry* 46 (1983): 312-32.
3. Elaine Carmen et al., "Victims of Violence and Psychiatric Illness," *American Journal of Psychiatry* 141, no. 3 (1984): 378-83.

TRICKED BY MEMORY

Elizabeth F. Loftus

Elizabeth Loftus is renowned as a courtroom specialist in eyewitness testimony, directly applying almost twenty years of psychological research on human memory. Loftus has compiled a comprehensive and profound body of work on eyewitness testimony centering on the question, How capable is the average person of storing and remembering information in detail? A professor of psychology and adjunct professor of law at the University of Washington, she focuses in this paper on the ways in which individual memory can be distorted through what she has called "red herrings," those "little bits of information that get into the memory system, float around, and cause trouble." Loftus is concerned with how individual memory works and responds in determining what really happened in a specific situation in a factual way. Her publications include Eyewitness Testimony *(1979),* Memory *(1980),* Eyewitness Testimony: Psychological Perspectives *(1984),* Eyewitness Testimony: Civil and Criminal *(1987), and* Witness for the Defense *(1991).*

It is always a matter of some fascination when human memory goes awry. It happened to President Ronald Reagan when he was tricked by his own changing memories of the Iran-Contra affair. On 26 January 1987, the President said that in August of 1985 he had approved the shipment of arms by Israel to Iran. He couldn't remember the precise date, but he did remember giving approval. By February 11, his memory had changed. Now, he said, after talking things over with his close advisor, Donald Regan, he did not recall authorizing the August shipment. President Reagan had gone over the matter several times with Mr. Regan, and specifically recalled that he was "surprised" to learn that the Israelis had shipped arms to Iran, and that this surprised feeling must have meant that he did not give advance approval for the transfer.

Later in February, Reagan tried to explain his changing memory: "In trying to recall the events that happened eighteen months ago, I'm afraid that I let myself be influenced by others' recollections, not my own. . . . I have no personal notes or records to help my recollection on this matter. The only honest answer is to say that try as I might, I cannot recall anything . . . the simple truth is, I don't remember—period."[1]

Reagan might take comfort in knowing of a body of research that shows that he is not alone. We all let ourselves be influenced by the recollections of others, even though we may not realize it. The memories of others can effectively invade us, like Trojan horses, precisely because we do not detect their influence. Understanding how we become tricked by memory is important, not only because memory is important to history, but because it is central to the way in which we identify ourselves.

Modern-day research showing how memory can become skewed (when people unwittingly assimilate new information) utilizes a simple paradigm. Subjects witness a complex event, like a film of a crime or an accident. Subsequently, some receive new, often misleading information about the event. Control subjects do not. Finally, all subjects attempt to recall the original event. In a typical example of a study using this paradigm, subjects saw a series of slides depicting a traffic accident. They then received written information about the accident, but some subjects were misled about what they saw. For example, a stop sign in the slides was referred to as a yield sign. When asked whether they originally saw a stop or a yield sign, the misled subjects performed much more poorly than controls.

This basic paradigm has been duplicated in scores of studies, involving a wide variety of materials.[2] When exposed to misleading postevent information, subjects have not only misrecalled stop signs as yield signs, but they have misrecalled the color of a car that was green as being blue, hammers as wrenches, straight hair as being curly, broken glass or tape recorders that never existed, and even recalled something as large and conspicuous as a barn when no barn was ever seen. In short, misleading postevent information can alter a person's recollection of an event. I refer to this phenomenon as the misinformation effect. Now that researchers have established the ubiquity of the misinformation effect, they are trying to understand its full nature. What does the misinformation effect tell us about the way memory works? Once misinformation has invaded memory, can the original memories ever be recovered? Are there any techniques that can be used to distinguish between a memory that is the result of true perception and a memory that is a result of suggestion?

THE IMPORTANCE OF MEMORY

Without memory, life would consist of momentary experiences that have little relation to one another. Without memory we could not communicate with other people for we could not remember the ideas we wished to express. Without memory, we would not have the sense of continuity even to know who we are. Memory is central to being human; thus

will come as no surprise that philosophers and scientists have been in-
erested in the subject as far back as recorded history goes.

How far back can we go? Greek mythology gave us a goddess of mem-
ry or remembrance—her name was Mnemosyne. Mnemosyne grants
ower through her daughters to "tell of what is, and what is to be, and
hat was before now."[3] In representing memory, Mnemosyne represented
e foundation of all intellectual discipline and wisdom. For some Greek
hilosophers, the goddess also paradoxically brought "forgetfulness of
orrow and rest from anxiety." This was a beneficent and creative forget-
ng. But for most of the philosophers of the day memory and forgetfulness
vere opposites. To lack memory was to lack knowledge and ultimately to
ose oneself.

Some of the most profound historical writing about memory occurred
luring the seventeenth century. In 1690, for example, John Locke distin-
uished between sensation and reflection—two sources or ideas in the
nind. For Locke, reflections consisted of thoughts about thoughts, and
hese could modify the simple sensory content of the mind that was
reated from perceiving a world of objects. Locke anticipated modern-day
esearch, then, when he talked about memory as a complex of sensory
deas modified by a history of reflection.

David Hume, a half century later, also recognized that our memories can
ontain both fact and fiction. In trying to distinguish the two, he sug-
ested that factual memory tends to be "more lively and strong" and
'paints its objects with more distinct colours." Thus, truth and falsehood
n memory have been enduring philosophical issues. Modern methods of
nvestigating memory developed from these roots. Eventually, history be-
ame the study of our collective memories, and psychology found a place
or itself as the scientific study of the human species in general, and individual memory in particular.

The experimental study of memory is at least one hundred years old.
For most of this period, the study of memory has been polarized. Early
psychologists such as Hermann Ebbinghaus were interested only in memory that was closely linked to sensory stimuli. They were not interested in
memory that was the result of reflective processes. Later-day psychologists
appreciated the idea that memory performance reflects not only pro-
gressive losses of information, but modifications as well. In fact, this
conception of memory became central to psychoanalytic theory and to the
work of many major theorists, such as Sir Francis Bartlett. Indeed, some of
these later scholars contended that all memory processes are reconstructive, meaning that retrieval of memory involves a process in which the
initial memory content is modified as a result of interactions with other
information already stored in memory.

But clearly some acts of remembering do not involve reconstructio
There is no indication that we reconstruct something when we rememb
our own name. No reconstruction seems to be involved when we remen
ber the arithmetic tables or the meaning of common words in our nativ
language or how to use a fork and knife to eat.

In short, our vast memory store contains different kinds of memories.
includes general knowledge about the world, such as the fact that AIDS i
a disease or that 4 x 5 is 20. But it also includes our own personal expe
riences, such as the conversation I had with a friend yesterday. These tw
kinds of memories might operate by a different set of laws. Indeed, in 197
University of Toronto psychologist Endel Tulving coined a usefu
distinction between the two classes of memories. He labeled the forme
kind "semantic memories" and the latter kind "episodic memories." In hi
own words:

> Episodic memory receives and stores information about temporall
> dated episodes or events, and temporal-spatial relations among thes
> events. . . . Semantic memory is necessary for the use of language. It is
> mental thesaurus, organized knowledge a person possesses abou
> words and other verbal symbols, their meaning and referents, abou
> relations among them, and about rules, formulas, and algorithms for th
> manipulation of these symbols, concepts and relations.[4]

In other words, episodic memory contains information about life expe
riences. It is memory of one's personal history—information that is asso
ciated with a particular time or place. Semantic memory has to do wit
one's general factual knowledge. Words and concepts that a perso
knows without necessarily knowing how or when they were firs
encountered or acquired fall into this category.

Tulving conceived of episodic and semantic memory as two information-processing systems that (1) selectively receive information from perceptual and cognitive systems, (2) retain various aspects of that information, and (3) transmit that information when it is needed. The two systems are thought to differ in terms of the type of information that is stored, the conditions and consequences of retrieval, and the possibility of their vulnerability to interference.

In his 1983 formulations, Tulving presented a much-expanded set of features that distinguish episodic and semantic memory. One important distinguishing feature is the vulnerability of information to change. Information stored in the episodic system is more vulnerable—it is changed, modified, and lost more readily—than information in the semantic system. Why? One reason is that the information in the semantic system is overarned while information in the episodic system is typically based upon ngle episodes.

In Tulving's formulation, there is clear recognition of the concept of the alleability of memory, at least as far as episodic memories are concerned. he idea that misleading information can enter a person's consciousness nd create havoc with previously acquired memories is implicit in this amework. The idea that memories can become altered has a place.

THE MALLEABILITY OF MEMORY

A variety of experiments have demonstrated the elasticity of memory. hrough suggestion, false memories have been created in the minds of eople for objects like barns and tape recorders that never existed. A umber of separate lines of research have tried to delimit the boundary onditions for the recollection change phenomenon. One line of research oncerns the delay interval between the initial experience and when misleading information is encountered. People are more influenced by misinformation when longer intervals of time occur after the initial event. nother line of research concerns the presence or absence of warnings. Vhen warned about the possibility of receiving misinformation, people are etter able to resist it. Apparently the warning motivates people to crutinize the misinformation, which leads to the greater likelihood of their letecting and then resisting the misinformation. These varied research ursuits concerning memory distortion are linked by a shared unifying rinciple known as "discrepancy detection." This refers to the detection f a conflict between the original memory and the misleading postevent nformation. A change in memory of an event is more likely to occur if liscrepancies between the original event and the misinformation are not mmediately detected.

THE FATE OF MEMORY

Although research on the misinformation effect is clear in showing that postevent information can influence a person's reported recollection, many questions remain as to why this occurs. Why is the postevent information remembered instead of what was originally experienced? A further question concerns the fate of the underlying memory traces. When a person sees an accident involving a car racing through an intersection with a red traffic light, and later "learns" that the light was green and now remembers seeing green, what happened to the original memory for a red light? Has the memory truly been updated or altered by the postevent in-

formation so that the original traces could not be recovered in the future
This has been referred to as the "alteration" hypothesis, and it sugges
that the original memory representations are altered when postevent in
formation is encoded that differs from what was originally experience
Another position is the "coexistence" hypothesis, which assumes that th
original and the postevent information coexist in memory. The introduc
tion of postevent information, under this position, is thought to make th
original memories simply less accessible, but still potentially recoverable
some future time.

The coexistence-alteration issue is important from both a theoretica
and a practical standpoint. Speaking practically, the dichotomy bears o
attempts that one might make to correct a memory after it has been biase
by postevent suggestion. Under the coexistence view, but perhaps not th
alteration view, it makes sense to vigorously pursue retrieval technique
(e.g., hypnosis, reinstatement of context) that might access the original in
formation. Under the alteration view, one's efforts would be placed else
where because it is likely that the only way to return to the origina
information is by a "re-alteration" of memory.

Theoretically speaking, the dichotomy bears on one of the most fun
damental questions about memory: the permanence of memory traces. Th
coexistence view is consistent with the idea that all information, onc
stored in memory, remains there more or less permanently. The alteratio
view implies a true loss of information from memory due to the updating
substitution, or blending in of new inputs.

Coexistence theories derive their support from studies that show suc
cessful recovery of original memories. Original memories have been suc
cessfully recovered, for example, by reinstating the context of the origina
event more fully, or by warning people that they may have been expose
to misleading information. Despite these successful recoveries of allegedly
altered memories, this still does not mean that all memories are similarly
recoverable.

Alteration theories derive their support (although are certainly not
proven) by numerous failed empirical attempts to recover original memory.
Even the mysterious technique of hypnosis has failed to lead to the
original memories once they have been altered. Of course, such failures do
not prove that the original memories do not exist, because it can always be
argued that the original memory does exist but that the appropriate retrieval method was not used or that the method used was not sufficiently
powerful.

Upon this intellectual battleground, there recently appeared some new
warriors who claim that neither the coexistence nor the alteration view
hold up. Michael McCloskey and Maria Zaragoza, from the psychology
department at Johns Hopkins University, maintain that misleading post-

vent information neither alters the original memory nor makes it less ccessible. Consider the empirical work that led them to this assertion.[6] he Hopkins researchers used the standard three-phase paradigm, with one odification. Subject was a simulated office burglary. The simulation ntained a number of critical items, one of which shows a man holding a ammer. Then subjects read a narrative describing the events shown in the ides. In the control condition, the narrative gave no specific information bout the critical item—it was referred to simply as a tool. In the misled ondition, the narrative referred to the critical item as a screwdriver. After ading the narrative, the subjects were tested on what they saw. The riginal test procedure required subjects to choose between hammer, the riginally seen item, and screwdriver, the item presented to the misled ubjects as misleading information.

The Hopkins researchers felt that this test was not adequate for telling hether the original memory has been modified since the postevent information could simply bias some subjects towards choosing the other object. So they created a modified procedure in which the bias presumably ould not operate. In the modified procedure, the misleading information, e screwdriver, was not included as an option on the test. Instead subjects ere asked to choose between the original item, the hammer, and a new em, a wrench. If misleading information impairs subjects' memories (by rasing the original or by making it less accessible), then misled subjects hould show poorer test performance than control subjects, even in the odified procedure. However, if misleading information does not influence emory for the original information, then control and misled conditions hould not differ.

The Hopkins researchers carried out six replications of this test using early eight hundred college students and found that misled and control ubjects performed about equally on recognition tests. They averaged 72 ercent and 75 percent correct, respectively. (With the traditional original rocedure—a test between hammer and screwdriver, for example—the esearchers obtained the usual effect of misleading information, 37 percent orrect for misled subjects and 72 percent correct for control subjects.) It vas these data that led the researchers to conclude that misleading information has no effect on a person's ability to remember the original event.

At the heart of the Hopkins work is the complaint that the usual testing rocedure, where the suggested item is included on the test, is inappropriate for assessing the effects of misleading information on memory. Yet he usual testing procedure is quite appropriate for answering certain kinds f questions about the misinformation effect. Consider a case in which ubjects see a man with a hammer. Later, some subjects receive misleading nformation about a screwdriver. How shall we now test these subjects to ssess the impact of postevent information? If we wanted to know

whether misled subjects would adopt the suggestion and choose it on
recognition test, it would be perfectly appropriate to give subjects a choi
between the original and suggested item.

But suppose that we were interested in whether the misleading infc
mation impaired memory. In this case, the Hopkins researchers may be rig
that the presence of the suggested item on the test and the choice b
subjects of that item cannot be easily interpreted. Subjects could b
choosing the item not because their memory is impaired but because the
feel that the experimenter wants them to or because they feel that the e
perimenter must know more than they do. Or they could choose the ite
because they failed to encode the original information and the misleadin
information supplemented their memory. Or, finally, they could b
choosing the item because their memory was altered by the misleading in
formation. Past researchers have recognized these possibilities before an
have used a variety of techniques to attempt to disentangle the various in
terpretations. In one study designed explicitly to identify those who we
simply succumbing to the experimenter's wishes or apparent knowledge,
was concluded that only a small percentage of misled subjects could b
characterized this way.

If the presence of the suggested item as a response possibility leads t
problems in interpreting performance, does the absence of the suggeste
item solve those problems? Certainly if subjects cannot choose the sug
gested item, then they cannot respond to that particular demand characte
istic. This is one apparent benefit of the modified test. However, there ar
other problems with the modified test that must be recognized. One prob
lem is that it is not sufficiently sensitive to detect small impairments i
memory. Put another way, the test between hammer and wrench (when th
suggested item was screwdriver) may not have been sensitive enough t
capture a loss in accessibility of hammer. This arises in part because man
subjects will simply guess when they do not know the right answer. Wit
the two-item test (hammer versus wrench), subjects can guess the corre
answer half the time. The particular items used in the Hopkins researc
were difficult items (as evidenced by the fact that the misled subjects wer
correct only 72 percent of the time). Thus they were not particularly ac
cessible even for subjects who were not misled. If items are not particularl
accessible to begin with, it is hard to make them less accessible. Thi
reasoning motivated research by Carla Chandler (1989).[7] Chandler foun
that when she utilized critical items that were indeed accessible to begi
with, misleading postevent information impaired memory performance eve
in a test that did not permit the choice of the misleading item.

Ultimately, the current debate regarding the most appropriate way t
conceptualize the rate of postevent information requires addressing som
critical questions about the nature of memory representation. Since w

annot get inside subjects' heads to see how their memories are repre-nted, we must rely on indirect inferences based on reports of what is re-alled. Unfortunately, what subjects claim to experience may not actually present the true nature of their memories. Even if we demonstrate that abjects truly believe that their altered memories represent what they iginally saw, we can never know whether somewhere in the recesses of e mind lies an inaccessible but pristine memory trace. Thus, rather than ying to make inferences about representation issues that may be unan-verable, researchers may more profitably shift the focus of research to ew questions. Under what conditions will we observe a change in mem-y performance after exposure to new information? Is there any way to istinguish a memory that results from a true perceptual experience from a emory that results from postevent suggestions? It is the latter question at I now address.

DISTINGUISHING REAL AND SUGGESTED MEMORIES

Some time ago I held a reception at my home for the president of the merican Psychological Association. The Armenian pinwheel sandwiches, rought by a caterer, were far better than anything I could have made ayself. So, it was with some sadness that I watched a plate of them acci-entally fall to the floor. The next day one of my colleagues mentioned the ity he felt at watching the fall of the plate of curried chicken puffs. A mild isagreement ensued over exactly what had fallen, and curiosity prompted ne to examine the trash, which proved the veracity of my version of the vent over his.

Why did my colleague misremember the fallen object as chicken puffs ather than pinwheel sandwiches? If I hadn't had a convenient way to erify these memories, would there have been some technique that I could ave used to probe my colleague's memory further and establish its eracity?

The problem of judging the reality of memory arises again and again. Vhen we listen to people describe events from their past, we make judg-nents about those descriptions. We judge whether or not the speaker is ying, perhaps using cues such as reduced eye contact or speech esitations to indicate a possible lie. But what if our speaker is trying to tell he truth? He might or might not be accurate. Can the average listener tell vhich memories are accurate and which are not? When Oliver North estified at the Iran-Contra hearings that the late CIA director William Casey had given him a ledger in which to record the flow of money to the Contras and at times this account contained as much as $175,000, was this

memory accurate? Could we examine North's words carefully and g
clues as to the veracity of the underlying memory?

Psychologist Marcia Johnson and her collaborators have investigatec
theory termed "reality monitoring" that accounts for how people disti
guish memory that results from a true perceptual experience from memo
that results from acts of imagination or from other nonreal memories.[8] T
representation of a true perception is thought to contain more spatial a
temporal attributes, more sensory attributes, and more detail. T
representation of nonreal memories are thought to contain more i
formation about the cognitive operations that produced these details. A
plying reality monitoring theory to my colleague's memory for chick
puffs, we might expect that, if asked to describe his memory, he mig
mention rather few sensory details, while emphasizing his own cogniti
processes (e.g., "I remember thinking to myself when the chicken puffs f
how I wished I had eaten another one before it happened"). In contras
someone who actually saw the pinwheels might be more apt to recall,
remember how funny shaped they became after they plopped on t
floor."

In collaboration with former students, I tested these predictions b
comparing the written descriptions of real and suggested memories. In o
study, subjects viewed a series of slides depicting a car accident. We ask
subjects who had either seen a car go through an intersection with a yie
sign, or who had merely had the yield sign suggested to them, to give
detailed description of the object. When examined one at a time, the re
and suggested descriptions were virtually indistinguishable from one a
other. Consider these verbatim descriptions:

1. As the car was approaching the intersection, I saw the yield sign a the corner.
2. It was on the corner on the right side of the street.
3. When the Datsun pulled up to the yield sign, it was there on the rig corner. It was a red and white triangle, not yellow.

Which descriptions came from subjects who actually saw the sign an
which came from subjects who simply had it suggested to them? Mo
people generally cannot tell. In reality, the first and third came from sub
jects who saw the sign while the second one came from a subject who ha
it created in his mind. We asked judges to tell us whether a particula
memory description came from someone who was accurate or inaccurat
Although the judges performed above chance levels, their ability to distin
guish was not particularly good.

Although it is difficult to classify correctly an individual description a
to its authenticity, when a large set of descriptions was analyzed, som

interesting results emerged. Real memory descriptions were more likely to explicitly mention the sensory properties of the sign. An example of a sign description that contained this quality is, "I saw the yield sign—it was red and white—looked like any old yield sign." Suggested memory descriptions were more likely to mention the thought processes that the subject engaged while watching the accident or while trying to recall it. An example of a description that contained this quality is, "After seeing the question, the answer I gave was more of an immediate impression of what I remembered. But I believe it was located on the corner just before the car turned."

Our research provides support for some of the earlier philosophical intuitions about the differences between veridical and nonveridical memories. However, we go further in identifying some of the characteristics that might typify these two classes of memories. In a wide variety of studies, we have shown that real and unreal memories are often associated with telltale verbal cues indicating their source. Real memory descriptions reflect more perceptual processing, including greater sensory detail. Suggested memories reflect more internal processing, including more mention of thought processes.

At this point it is important to acknowledge that the memory descriptions used in the research just described were written down by subjects rather than spoken out loud. Perhaps if subjects were allowed to naturally describe through speaking the contents of their memories, more information would be available to use for judging the probable veracity of the underlying memory. In a study to assess this possibility, subjects were videotaped while they described out loud various objects they claimed to have seen from a previously presented simulated burglary. Before the videotaped recall session, some subjects received misleading postevent information about certain critical details, and others did not.

Once again, the real descriptions tended to include more sensory details and the suggested description contained more information about cognitive processes. When judges watched the videotapes to see if they could tell when a subject was describing a real memory and when the memory was the result of suggestion, the judges did not perform well. When they heard a subject describe a nonexistent blue robe hanging on the wall of the bathroom, they were nearly as convinced that the object really existed as when they heard a subject who described a blue bathrobe that he had actually seen. Judges tended to believe that witnesses had seen what they claimed, whether it was true or not.

In several studies, then, untrained judges could not readily distinguish real and unreal memories. Can they be helped, in any way, to better perform this task? Fortunately, it appears that they can. When we told judges exactly what to look for, their ability improved. More specifically, when we provided judges with information (hints) regarding the differences between suggested and real memories, their ability to gauge the accuracy of someone else's memory significantly improved. The hints that we gave judges to use were quite straightforward: Look for examples of sensory details, look for instances of mentioning cognitive operations, and so on.

Before one becomes overly tempted to use this advice to make assessments of whether a particular memory is real or not, caution is in order. Many nonreal memories contain lots of detail. The astonishingly detailed memory of one man, John Dean, provides the perfect example. Recall that Dean was former counsel to President Richard Nixon during the Watergate break-in. In June 1973, Dean testified before a committee of the United States Senate, and he began his testimony with a 245-page statement describing dozens of meetings that he had attended with various other persons on Nixon's staff over the previous several years. Because Dean's memory was so detailed, several senators disbelieved Dean's memory. One asked Dean, "Have you always had a facility for recalling the details of conversations which took place many months ago?" The senator was especially impressed that Dean had done this without the benefit of notes or a daily diary.

Dean said he kept a newspaper clipping file from the date of the first *Washington Post* article until the time of the Senate hearings. He said he triggered his recollection by reading every single newspaper article, outlining what happened, and then placing himself in the described scene.

Did the articles trigger his recollection, as Dean claimed, or did they partially supplement or distort his memory? Dean was unaware that all conversations in Nixon's Oval Office were secretly recorded. Psychologist Ulric Neisser, who made an extensive comparison of those tapes with Dean's Senate testimony, concluded that Dean was entirely wrong about the course of many conversations, but nevertheless he essentially recounted the facts of those conversations.[10] Although it is difficult to ascertain whether Dean truly remembered those facts or whether he reinstated those facts into his memory from his perusal of newspaper clippings, it is of interest that his excessive detail prompted disbelief in those charged with judging his memory.

Most judges, like the senators judging Dean, are not especially good at discriminating real and suggested memories. In Dean's case, his excessive detail led people to disbelieve him, although in most cases, detail is impressive in a positive way. Could judges be given information that would allow them to make a more accurate determination of whether a memory description is real or not? Some promising new work suggests that providing judges with certain hints improves their ability to tell when someone has been tricked by memory. Far more research is needed to really develop the ability to tell in ourselves, as well as in others, which memories are real and which are not.

Notes

1. John Tower, Edmund Muskie, Brent Scowcroft, eds., *Report of the President's Special Review Board* (Washington, D.C.: U.S. Government Printing Office, 26 February 1987), 819-20.

2. See Elizabeth F. Loftus, *Eyewitness Testimony* (Cambridge, Mass.: Harvard University Press, 1979); and Elizabeth F. Loftus and Katherine Ketcham, *Witness for the Defense: The Accused, the Eyewitness, and the Expert Who Puts Memory on Trial* (New York: St. Martin's Press, 1991).

3. Hesiod, *Theogony*, trans. Richmond Lattimore (Ann Arbor: University of Michigan Press, 1984), quoted in M. Lourie, D. Stenton, and M. Vicinus, eds., "Women and Memory," *Michigan Quarterly Review* 26, no. 1:1.

4. Endel Tulving, "Episodic and Semantic Memory," in *Organization of Memory*, ed. Endel Tulving and Wayne Donaldson (New York: Academic Press, 1977), 385-86.

5. Endel Tulving, *Elements of Episodic Memory* (New York: Oxford University Press, 1983).

6. Michael McClosky and Maria Zaragosa, "Misleading Postevent Information and Memory for Events: Arguments and Evidence Against Memory Impairment Hypotheses," *Journal of Experimental Psychology: General* 114 (1): 1-16.

7. C. C. Chandler, "Specific Retroactive Interference in Modified Recognition Tests: Evidence for an Unknown Cause of Interference," *Journal of Experimental Psychology: Learning, Memory & Cognition* 15 (1989): 256-65.

8. M. K. Johnson and C. L. Raye, "Reality Monitoring," *Psychological Review* 88 (1981): 67-85.

9. J. W. Schooler, D. Gerhard, and E. F. Loftus, "Qualities of the Unreal," *Journal of Experimental Psychology: Learning, Memory & Cognition* 12 (1986): 171-81.

10. Ulric Neisser, "John Dean's Memory: A Case Study" in *Memory Observed: Remembering in Natural Contexts*, ed. Ulric Neisser (San Francisco: W. H. Freeman, 1982), 139-59.

COMMENT

Eva M. McMahan *teaches speech communications at the University of Alabama. Author of* Elite Oral History Discourse: A Study of Cooperation and Coherence, *she here applies insights from her own specialty of discourse analysis to Loftus's psychological research, discussing particularly the relationships involved in oral history and oral history as a creative process.*

Since my discipline is speech communication, I want to discuss the relationship between Elizabeth Loftus's memory research and the interview process of oral history. The link that I am seeking to address is found in the creation of historical records, a creative process in which memory and discourse are inextricably bound.

There are two relationships within this creative process which parallel two themes highlighted by Loftus. The first I label the synchronic communicative experience of the oral interview. The second is the diachronic relationship between the interactants and the historical event.[1]

Turning to the synchronic communicative experience, we see the most direct connection to Loftus's work on postevent contamination, that is, new information that people unwittingly incorporate into their previously stored memories. Loftus's research convincingly demonstrates the malleability of human memory, even in the context of short-lived recollection exercises. Since researchers can rather easily induce postevent contamination, it stands to reason that oral history interviewers can also induce postevent contamination, albeit unwittingly.

I define oral history as a conversation with a person whose life experience is regarded as memorable. This conversation, however, cannot be regarded as comparable to other documentary modes of inquiry. This is because the interview is an investigative form in which evidence originates through oral, face-to-face communication. The oral history interview is the joint intellectual product of a process wherein understanding is aided through speech and counterspeech. The interpretative acts of remembering, thinking, and speaking signify the meaning which emerges through the speech performances. Clearly, Loftus's work alerts us to the interpretative act of remembering and to the potential influences of the oral interview method on the recollection process.

For example, the research suggests that syntax and word choice in interviewer discourse can be quite influential in remembering. Apparently, interviewers can contaminate respondent memories by embedding discrepant information into minor clauses of questions. It also appears that forewarning could be used as a preventative for certain types of bias. While Loftus has not tested these ideas in the context of the oral history interview, I certainly would like to see such work taking place.

In a similar vein, Loftus's research alerts us to other forms of potential postevent contamination which are relevant for oral history. We live in an

Information Age where people are more likely than not to encounter printed and video versions of historical events, not to mention endless discussions of said events by pundits and other commentators. I would like to see the imagination and experimental rigor of Loftus focused on questions of how the activity of oral recollection impacts on the memories that are preserved. For example, my colleagues at the University of Alabama are working on the history of the desegregation of the university. The first desegregation attempt occurred in 1956 when Autherine Lucy, a young black woman, was admitted to the university. Riots erupted on campus. Recounting events during that four-day period, several townspeople claim to remember picking up Ms. Lucy at the city jail. Actually, it was Lucy's driver who was picked up. We need to know more about how the processes of remembering, thinking, and speaking influence accurate and inaccurate memories.

For me, the most intriguing aspect of Loftus's work pertains to the diachronic relationship in the oral history interview: the relationship between the interactants and the historical event. She argues that memory researchers should conceptualize human memory in new ways, noting that memories are not neat photos containing only the original or only the suggested information, but are more like montages containing a variety of features blended into a holistic representation.

I believe such a holistic characterization of memory is the most fruitful conceptual grounding for those who are interested in memory and history. Clearly, this depiction of memory would enable us to explore the diachronic relationship between the interactants and the historical event. As a researcher, the oral historian brings her or his informed perspective of the historical event, for example, the knowledge that Lucy's driver was picked up downtown. Even so, that perspective is, as Joseph Kockelmans would note, a reflection of the "historicity of historical interpretation."[2] The historian's viewpoint, then, is the product of the evolution of historical tradition which is itself "a succession of synchronic moments"[3] of remembering, thinking, and speaking.

While the relationship between the *respondent* and the historical event is also diachronic in nature, the respondent brings her or his own perception of that event formed from the memory of lived-through experience; that is, townspeople who recall picking up Lucy instead of her driver. Since any lived experience can acquire meaning only to the extent that it is reflected upon after it occurs, the interviewee's knowledge of the event develops diachronically.[4] The meaning of the lived experience depends upon the "temporal distance" of the interviewee. "Temporal distance is not a distance to be traveled through," notes Kockelmans, "but a living continuity of elements which as links in a chain constitute the tradition which functions as the light in which everything with which we are confronted . . . can appear as that which it really is."[5] Storytelling, as discussed by Daniel Bertaux, is illustrative. Bertaux says, "Stories about the past are told from the present, from a situation which may have changed over the years and defines a new relationship to the past. It is this relationship which underlies the whole story. . . . Telling a story about the past is a way of expressing indirectly a meaning about the present."[6]

Finally, the interdependent relationships among interviewers, interviewee, and the historical event reflect the holistic and complex nature of the oral history interview situation. This hermeneutical situation is both synchronic and diachronic and, as such, directs attention to the jointly creative process wherein historical meanings are produced. The production of that meaning is bound to the interpretative acts of remembering, thinking, and speaking. Therefore, among other things, we need to know how the act of oral interviewing impacts on memories; how the act of reflection influences those memories; how the act of articulation solidifies memories; what kinds of memories are best obtained through oral interviewing; and how interview context influences memory.

Because these synchronic and diachronic relationships are inherent in the hermeneutical situation of the oral history interview, I believe memory research which is pursued from the holistic viewpoint supported by Loftus can provide much needed insights into the relationships among oral interviewing, memory, and history.

Notes

1. E. Culpepper Clark, Michael J. Hyde, and Eva M. McMahan, "Communication in the Oral History Interview: Investigating Problems of Interpreting Oral Data," *International Journal of Oral History* 1 (February 1980): 28-40.
2. Joseph J. Kockelmans, "Toward An Interpretative or Hermeneutic Social Science," *New School for Social Research Graduate Faculty Philosophy Journal* 5 (Fall 1975): 83.
3. Clark, Hyde, and McMahan, "Communication," 32.
4. Ibid.
5. Kockelmans, "Interpretative or Hermeneutic," 92.
6. Daniel Bertaux, "Stories as Clues to Sociological Understanding: The Bakers of Paris," in *Our Common History: The Transformation of Europe*, ed. Paul Thompson (London: Pluto Press, 1982), 98.

AMERICAN HISTORY AND THE STRUCTURES OF COLLECTIVE MEMORY: A MODEST EXERCISE IN EMPIRICAL ICONOGRAPHY

Michael H. Frisch

Michael H. Frisch is a professor of history and the chair of the American Studies Department at the State University of New York at Buffalo, specializing in urban, social, and cultural history. His oral projects on labor and society and iron and steel workers are explored in his books Working-Class America *(1983) and* Portraits in Steel *(1993). He is editor of the* Oral History Review *and author of* A Shared Authority: Essays on the Craft and Meaning of Oral and Public History *(1991). In this paper Frisch draws on his experience in the classroom to examine cultural memory in the United States and how that memory has been observed—indeed, measured—in American education. Known for his innovative approach to scholarship and fearless mixing of the sacred with the profane, here he grapples with the functionalist view of cultural memory, with fluidity versus stability of "historical truth."*

For over a decade now, I have been accumulating some fascinating data bearing on the images of American history that my students have carried around in their heads before entering my classroom. The term *data* may be misleadingly scientific, and I'm not even sure my hunting and gathering process deserves to be called research, since it began playfully, little more than a tonic designed to fortify student recruits setting out on their uncertain trek across the arid reaches of the standard survey course. Increasingly, however, I have come to sense that there may be some broader meaning, or at least interest, in the picture gradually emerging through this experimentation.

This sense has been recently sharpened by loud alarums—the very lively debate about American education's role in the ominously accelerating historical amnesia reportedly afflicting high-school and college students. As it happens, my modest experiments in what can be called "empirical iconography," conducted well before this debate emerged, address its concerns quite directly, providing a certain reassurance in the face of the jeremiads, while raising some disturbing questions of rather a different sort.

Let me begin with some brief form-setting observations about the problem at hand. I will then turn to a straightforward unfolding of my quasi-scientific data combined with some unlicensed flights of exegetical excess. I will conclude by returning to the contemporary debate about American education and historical memory, in order to see how different it may appear after our excursion into the realm of the collective historical subconscious, or at least that portion of it embodied in the responses of some seven hundred students at the State University of New York at Buffalo over the past decade.

As a general matter, discussions of historical memory have not been very clear about the relation of individual-level processes—what and how we remember, whether about our own or more broadly historical experience—and the processes of collective memory, those broader patterns through which culture may shape the parameters, structure, and even the content of our sense of history. My impression is the two levels of discussion have remained relatively separate, the first engaged more by those concerned with psychology, education, language, and to an extent oral history, the latter by cultural historians.

The current debate about history, culture, and education in American life has brought these differing aspects of memory together, focusing as it does on what individuals know about history, how they come to know (or not know) it, and what this says about our collective culture, in terms of both cause and broader effect. I will presume a certain familiarity with the recently discovered crisis of cultural illiteracy, which certainly seems to have struck a genuine chord of some kind. Two basic texts by the prophets Allan Bloom and E. D. Hirsch, Jr., have been improbable best sellers for many months, and there has been widespread discussion of documents such as "A Nation at Risk," the report of the National Commission of Excellence in Education, and "American Memory: A Report on the Humanities in the Nation's Public Schools," by National Endowment for the Humanities chairman Lynne Cheney. These have all worked their way into newsweekly cover stories and extensive TV news coverage as well. The most recent sensation, Diane Ravitch and Chester I. Finn's *What Do Our 17-Year-Olds Know?*, has seemed to offer the hard epidemiological evidence on which the declaration of a cultural health emergency has been based.[1]

This literature is far from uniform, but for present purposes it is possible to identify at least three linked propositions sounded consistently in all these works, and others in the same vein. The first, already noted, is that our students and young adults are woefully ignorant of the most basic orienting facts of history, particularly our own American history, much less its larger meanings, with the result that the strings of a shared cultural memory have been cut. The second proposition is that this severing of memory is a direct consequence of a failure of education, of the diminished place of history education in the curriculum at every level, and of a deterioration in the pedagogy by which we teach whatever history has managed to survive. The final proposition, a derivative of the first two, is that unless there is a drastic change in the quantity and quality of the teaching of history, the only issue will be whether we collapse from internal disintegration before we are overwhelmed by economic and political threats from without. Indeed, the most apocalyptic critics mirror the homophobic right in its view of AIDS, seeing the amnesia epidemic as at once a threat to our survival and a kind of divine judgment on a culture gone wrong.

These propositions all involve history and memory, and all turn out, on close examination, to be something short of self-evident, at least in the sense in which they are usually advanced. The last mentioned, of course, is so dependent on a particular ideological worldview as to be beyond the critical discussion appropriate in this forum. The first two, however, are as statements more objective in form, and amenable to both internal and external test.

The evidence I present here is offered in this spirit. As for the first, root proposition, my data challenge the amnesiac conclusion itself, quite directly. While my tables can lay claim to little scientific validity, in at least one respect they address the central question more squarely than most of the well-funded research on which the current debate rests. Ravitch and Finn's title notwithstanding, the major survey work has pursued a kind of inversion of Howard Baker's famous Watergate Query: What Don't the Students Know and Since When Haven't They Known It? But to answer this, even assuming the dubious validity of the survey instrument, is not necessarily to discover the other side of the coin, to see and understand what they *do* know.[2] However inadvertently, my somewhat whimsical investigation may have stumbled on some very different results because it began as an attempt to map that very terrain, to explore an interior historical landscape exactly as presented by students.

In fact, the expedition has revealed an environment so strikingly uniform as to cast a significant shadow over the remaining proposition—that pedagogy and curriculum are critical variables in the structuring of "American Memory." My evidence suggests that our students' historical memory may not, in fact, be shaped so much by their education or lack of it as by collective cultural mechanisms and structures we need better to understand. In this sense, the research bears quite directly on a central focus of recent cultural studies, the concept of "Civil Religion." This argues the existence in American culture of the set of shared beliefs, myths, "meaning systems," and historical images that can be said to have essentially religious structure, and inquires into the content, origins, and functions of this complex, both as a general cultural concept and in terms of its particular American meaning.[3]

Because so much prior discussion has relied on literary rather than empirical evidence of the very existence, much less shared acceptance, of such core cultural beliefs, my data may help advance this inquiry. Cultural analysis, in turn, has much to contribute to an interdisciplinary focus on the relation of history to memory. Unless we can bring these far from identical concepts together in a clearly demarcated arena, we will have difficulty penetrating an increasingly strident public discourse in which they are being pressed into the dubious service of some not-so-hidden agendas. But approached with careful curiosity and the conceptual tools commonly found in our scholarly workshops, it may be possible to get closer to the core of legitimate concern in this debate. Even more, I believe this may be one of the rare instances where the benefits flow both ways—where the heat of a particular polemic can generate light sufficient to illuminate some of the issues.

First let me describe my classroom laboratory. Over a decade ago, I was first assigned to take my turn lecturing the first semester of our standard year-long American history survey course, from the beginning through the Civil War. As one who had been teaching the relatively exotic specialty of urban and social history, I realized that this would be my initiation teaching materials that most of my students had previously encountered, in what I presumed to be high-school versions, parochial at best and grossly distorted at the expected worst. With all the arrogance of a beginner, I expected my major task would be redemptive, the clearing of a forest of facts, names, dates, and conventional concepts in order to build, out of the logs of American experience, a city of insight and understanding.

As a way to survey the wilderness before me, I began the very first class with a spot quiz: I asked the students to take out blank paper, and to write down, without undue reflection, the first ten names that popped into their heads in response to the prompt "American history from its beginnings through the end of the Civil War." Assuming that the lists would be predictably presidential, starting with George Washington, after the students had finished I suggested that the experiment be repeated, but this time excluding presidents, generals, statesmen, or other figures in official public life. I hoped that the two lists in combination would be a reasonable approximation of the image of American history brought into the class. The quiz was anonymous, I assured them, simply a way to obtain, via free association, a kind of collective portrait of our starting point. My intention was to fashion, out of the collated answers, an opening lecture contrasting this high-school image to the university-level alternative we would develop during the semester.

The results were in some ways quite surprising, which encouraged me to repeat the quizzes each time I have taught the course. I have now run seven such surveys, between 1975 and 1985, involving over 700 students in groups ranging from 40 to 170. This is a sufficiently substantial base, I think, to justify taking a close look at the results.

Tables 1.1 and 1.2 present the two most recent surveys' tally for the first question. The parenthetic figures are the number of students mentioning each name. (About 95 took the quiz in 1984 and 170 in 1985). I should note that the free-association mechanism worked dramatically: many students listed only five or six names and then froze, their minds a blank, although they realized on seeing the lists later that they "knew" virtually every name anybody had mentioned. It is, of course, the difference between those names recognized and those immediately leaping to mind that students of culture, with backing from the psychologists, may find most interesting. The phenomenon helps compensate as well for a methodological deficiency: in a more serious analysis, it would be important to analyze the order of mention as well as the frequency, but as this was beyond my statistical resources, I sought an approximation by limiting the time available and by encouraging students to stop when their minds began to go blank, rather than to fill up all ten places through more deliberate concentration.

These first tables are unsurprising, a combination of mostly political and military figures crystallized around the major defining events of U.S. history, the Revolution and the Civil War. There is little here to suggest anything other than the dutiful, civic-focused high-school history courses whose residue I had expected to find. But as we shall see, the other results cast the lists in a somewhat different light.

Table 1.3 presents a seven-time comparison of answers to this question. The lists are of unequal length because each survey rank orders all those names receiving at least three to six mentions; wherever it falls ordinally, the last name marks a dropping-off point, with all others below it receiving only relatively isolated mentions.

The results confirm the initial impression of any one year, but the uniformity is quite striking. Considering first the "top ten" of each list, we find six names appearing every year (Washington, Jefferson, Lincoln, Ulysses S. Grant, John Adams, and Benjamin Franklin). As charted in Table 1.4, six other names rank in the top ten five of the seven years: Robert E. Lee, Paul Revere, James Madison, John Hancock, Andrew Jackson, and Alexander Hamilton.

All told, only fourteen different names appear in the seventy slots (ten each year for seven years) at the top of the lists. To be in social-scientific

Table 1.1

Question One Tally: 1984

(Question One: Write down the first ten names that you think of in response to the prompt, "American History from its beginning through the end of the Civil War.")

Class Responses [Frequency of Inclusion]:

Rank	*Name*	*Frequency*	*Rank*	*Name*	*Frequency*
1	G. Washington	83	21	T. Paine	5
2	A. Lincoln	76	22	J. Davis	4
3	T. Jefferson	70	23	N. Hale	4
4	B. Franklin	52	24	J. Monroe	4
5	R. E. Lee	37	25	B. Arnold	3
6	U. S. Grant	31	26	J. Cabot	3
7	J. Adams	30	27	Cornwallis	3
8	C. Columbus	22	28	G. A. Custer	3
9	P. Revere	22	29	George III	3
10	J. Hancock	16	30	Lafayette	3
11	J. Smith	10	31	Magellan	3
12	A. Jackson	9	32	S. Adams	2
13	J. Q. Adams	7	33	D. Boone	2
14	J. W. Booth	7	34	A. Burr	2
15	A. Hamilton	7	35	H. Clay	2
16	B. Ross	7	36	T. Edison	2
17	P. Henry	6	37	F. S. Key	2
18	J. Madison	6	38	D. Madison	2
19	S. Jackson	5	39	Pocahontas	2
20	Lewis & Clark	5	40	H. Tubman	2

fashion, I have calculated measures of the diversity and consensus on these lists (Table 1.5). The maximum number of possible top-ten names (seventy) minus the minimum possible (ten) yields a maximum "spread" of sixty. Subtracting from the actual total number of names in the seventy slots (fourteen) that same minimum (ten) yields an *actual* spread of four. To provide a standardized base for comparison, dividing actual spread by the potential maximum yields an index on a scale where 0.00 represents total lack of diversity (the same ten names each year) and 1.00 represents

Table 1.2
Question One Tally: 1985

(Question One: Write down the first ten names that you think of in response to the prompt, "American History from its beginning through the end of the Civil War.")

Class Responses [Frequency of Inclusion]:

Rank	*Name*	*Frequency*	*Rank*	*Name*	*Frequency*
1	G. Washington	157	27	S. Jackson	6
2	A. Lincoln	129	28	F. S. Key	6
3	T. Jefferson	124	29	T. Paine	6
4	J. Adams	94	30	W. T. Sherman	6
5	B. Franklin	89	31	S. Douglas	5
6	U. S. Grant	54	32	Pocahontas	5
7	P. Revere	54	33	H. Clay	4
8	R. E. Lee	51	34	G. Custer	4
9	A. Jackson	43	35	A. Johnson	4
10	J. Hancock	33	36	J. P. Jones	4
11	C. Columbus	26	37	W. Penn	4
12	A. Hamilton	19	38	S. B. Anthony	3
13	J. Madison	19	39	F. Pierce	3
14	J. Smith	15	40	J. Polk	3
15	J. Q. Adams	13	41	N. Turner	3
16	George III	13	42	M. Washington	3
17	J. Monroe	12	43	E. Whitney	3
18	B. Ross	12	44	J. Buchanan	2
19	J. W. Booth	11	45	T. Edison	2
20	S. Adams	8	46	L. Erikson	2
21	B. Arnold	8	47	J. Jay	2
22	Lewis & Clark	8	48	D. Madison	2
23	H. Tubman	8	49	M. Standish	2
24	A. Burr	7	50	J. Tyler	2
25	J. Davis	7	51	A. Vespucci	2
26	P. Henry	7			

Table 1.3
Question One: Seven Samples

1975	1976	1978	1982
1. Washington	1. Washington	1. Washington	1. Washington
2. Jefferson	2. Jefferson	2. Jefferson	2. Lincoln
3. Lincoln	3. Lincoln	3. Lincoln	3. Jefferson
4. Grant	4. Franklin	4. Franklin	4. Franklin
5. Lee	5. J. Adams	5. Grant	5. J. Adams
6. J. Adams	6. Grant	6. Lee	6. Grant
7. Franklin	7. Revere	7. J. Adams	7. Jackson
8. Madison	8. Hancock	8. Jackson	8. Hancock
9. Hamilton	9. Jackson	9. Columbus	9. Lee
10. J. Smith	10. Hamilton	10. Revere	10. Revere
11. Columbus	11. Lee	11. Hancock	11. Madison
12. Ross	12. Ross	12. J. Smith	12. Columbus
13. Revere	13. P. Henry	13. George III	13. Custer
	14. Madison	14. Madison	14. Paine
	15. Columbus	15. Arnold	15. Hamilton

1983	1984	1985
1. Washington	1. Washington	1. Washington
2. Lincoln	2. Lincoln	2. Lincoln
3. Jefferson	3. Jefferson	3. Jefferson
4. Franklin	4. Franklin	4. J. Adams
5. Grant	5. Lee	5. Franklin
6. Lee	6 Grant	6. Grant
7. J. Adams	7. J. Adams	7. Revere
8. Hancock	8. Columbus	8. Lee
9. Revere	9. Revere	9. Jackson
10. Jackson	10. Hancock	10. Hancock
11. Columbus	11. J. Smith	11. Columbus
12. Madison	12. Jackson	12. Hamilton
13. Hamilton	13. J. Q. Adams	13. Madison
14. Monroe	14. J. W. Booth	14. J. Smith
15. J. P. Jones	15. Hamilton	15. J. Q. Adams
16. Custer	16. Ross	16. George III
17. P. Henry	17. P. Henry	17. Monroe
	18. Madison	18. Ross
		19. J. W. Booth

Table 1.4

Question One Seven Sample Summary

(Question One: Write down the first ten names that you think of in response to the prompt, "American History from its beginning through the end of the Civil War.")

	Rank in Year:							
Name	*1975*	*1976*	*1978*	*1982*	*1983*	*1984*	*1985*	*Years on List*
1 G. Washington	1	1	1	1	1	1	1	7
2 A. Lincoln	3	3	3	2	2	2	2	7
3 T. Jefferson	2	2	2	3	3	3	3	7
4 B. Franklin	7	4	4	4	4	4	5	7
5 U. S. Grant	4	6	5	6	5	6	6	7
6 J. Adams	6	5	7	5	7	7	4	7
7 R. E. Lee	5	11	6	9	6	5	8	7
8 P. Revere	13	7	10	10	9	9	7	7
9 C. Columbus	11	15	9	12	11	8	11	7
10 J. Madison	8	14	14	11	12	18	13	7
11 J. Hancock		8	11	8	8	10	10	6
12 A. Jackson		9	8	7	10	12	9	6
13 A. Hamilton	9	10		15	13	15	12	6
14 J. Smith	10		12			11	14	4
15 B. Ross	12	12				16	18	4
16. P. Henry		13			17	17		3
17 J. Q. Adams						13	15	2
18 George III			13				16	2
19 G. A. Custer				13	16			2
20 J. Monroe					14		17	2
21 J. W. Booth						14	19	2
22 T. Paine				14				1
23 B. Arnold			15					1
24 J. P. Jones					15			1

total diversity (no names appearing on more than one year's list.) This I will declare, only slightly tongue-in-cheek, to be the Diversity Index: for Question One's top ten, it is a minuscule .067.

The Consensus Index is less complex—those names appearing *every* year in the top ten as a percentage of all the names appearing *any* year in the top ten: 42.9 percent. Perhaps more indicative is Five Plus

Table 1.5
Seven Sample Analysis

Question One	*Top Ten*	*TTL List*
A. Total names	14	24
B. Maximum Possible Names	70	112
C. Minimum Possible Names	10	19
D. Maximum Possible Spread [B-C]	60	93
E. Actual Spread [A-C]	4	5
F. Diversity Index [E/D]	0.067	0.054
G. Names on List All Seven Years	6	10
H. Seven Year Consensus Index [G/A]	42.9%	41.7%
I. Names on List Five Years or More	12	13
J. Five Plus Consensus Index [I/A]	85.7%	54.2%
K. Consensus Decay Index [(J.1-J.2)/J.1]		0.37

Consensus Index: 85.7 percent of the names that ever appear in the t
ten did so in five or more of the seven years surveyed.

Moving from the top ten to consider the full lists, we find slots for 1
names, but only 24 different ones appearing, resulting in the Diversity I
dex of .054—slightly *lower* than that for the top ten. This is an importa
indication that the degree of diversity does not increase as one procee
down the list. Of these 24 names, 12 (41.7 percent) appear every year a
13 (54.2 percent) in five of the seven years. Both Diversity and Consens
indexes, then, suggest that the overall similarity of the lists is hard
accounted for by the very famous names at the top, but spreads relative
evenly through the full range of names my students mention on these lis
year after year.

Perhaps the most culturally revealing characteristic of the lists is the
near-exclusive political/military cast and its focus on epochal events.
class discussion, we have frequently noted the kinds of people missin
from the survey: religious figures, artists, philosophers, or scientists. It
hard to imagine a similar poll in England or Italy or China or Chile bein
quite so relentlessly political, public, and heroic. This certainly seemed
say something about American culture, but it is not inconsistent with m
original expectation that what I was measuring was the result of hig
school history curricula focused on our civic traditions and formal inst
tutions. The dramatic uniformity from year to year, however, suggeste
something else—perhaps an unexpected level of indoctrination or

Table 2.1
Question Two Tally: 1984

(Question One: Write down the first ten names that you think of, EXCLUDING PRESIDENTS, GENERALS, ET CETERA, in response to the prompt, "American History from its beginning through the end of the Civil War.")

Class Responses [Frequency of Inclusion]:

Rank	*Name*	*Frequency*	*Rank*	*Name*	*Frequency*
1	B. Ross	37	19	A. G. Bell	3
2	P. Revere	25	20	G. W. Carver	3
3	H. Tubman	15	21	F. Douglass	3
4	Lewis & Clark	14	22	J. Hancock	3
5	J. W. Booth	11	23	W. Penn	3
6	D. Madison	10	24	M. Standish	3
7	J. Smith	10	25	M. Washington	3
8	F. S. Key	8	26	S. B. Anthony	2
9	Pocahontas	8	27	C. Attucks	2
10	H. B. Stowe	7	28	A. Burr	2
11	D. Boone	6	29	D. Crockett	2
12	T. Edison	6	30	N. Hale	2
13	B. Franklin	6	31	C. McCormick	2
14	R. Fulton	6	32	F. Nightingale	2
15	B. Arnold	5	33	T. Paine	2
16	C. Barton	5	34	M. Pitcher	2
17	J. Brown	5	35	Sacajawea	2
18	J. P. Jones	4	36	D. Scott	2

deeper set of cultural structures at work on the collective imagination of students year after year.

The results of the second set of surveys offer some powerful evidence for the latter hypothesis and some provocative suggestions as to the content and meaning of those cultural structures. The most recent surveys are presented in Tables 2.1 and 2.2, a compendium of near-legendary characters who most Americans encounter in grade school, if anywhere on the educational spectrum; more generally, the figures on the list are the stuff of popular culture rather than school curricula.

Table 2.2
Question Two Tally: 1985

(Question One: Write down the first ten names that you think of, EXCLUDING PRESIDENTS, GENERALS, ET CETERA, in response to the prompt, "American History from its beginning through the end of the Civil War.")

Class Responses [Frequency of Inclusion]:

Rank	*Name*	*Frequency*	*Rank*	*Name*	*Frequency*
1	B. Ross	43	30	H. Clay	4
2	P. Revere	35	31	F. Douglass	4
3	H. Tubman	21	32	J. Hancock	4
4	C. Columbus	19	33	H. Hudson	4
5	F. S. Key	16	34	W. Penn	4
6	J. Smith	16	35	R. Fulton	3
7	Pocahontas	14	36	J. Henry	3
8	Lewis & Clark	13	37	J. McCormick	3
9	E. Whitney	13	38	W. Raleigh	3
10	B. Franklin	11	39	D. Scott	3
11	J. W. Booth	9	40	Sitting Bull	3
12	T. Paine	9	41	A. Vespucci	3
13	M. Washington	9	42	A. Adams	2
14	C. Attucks	7	43	A. Burr	2
15	J. Brown	7	44	A. Doubleday	2
16	G. W. Carver	7	45	J. Jay	2
17	S. B. Anthony	6	46	J. P. Jones	2
18	D. Boone	6	47	K. Kinte	2
19	N. Hale	6	48	J. Marshall	2
20	P. Henry	6	49	F. Nightingale	2
21	M. Pitcher	6	50	E. A. Poe	2
22	M. Standish	6	51	Red Jacket	2
23	H. B. Stowe	6	52	Squanto	2
24	B. Arnold	5	53	P. Stuyvesant	2
25	A. G. Bell	5	54	H. Thoreau	2
26	D. Crockett	5	55	J. Tremain	2
27	T. Edison	5	56	S. Truth	2
28	D. Madison	5	57	M. Twain	2
29	N.Turner	5	58	Duke of York	2

I must admit that the first time I encountered such results, I was quite surprised. Indeed, the students were surprised and a little embarrassed themselves: again, they all claimed to "know" something about the more sophisticated mentioned even once. Yet it seemed clear that when confronting the blank page, many of them had reached back beyond their more recent experience and listed figures imaginatively encountered a good bit earlier, or outside of school altogether.

This impression is confirmed, to put it mildly, by comparing the answers to this second survey in the five different years—results presented in Table 2.3. The lists are so consistent in character, and even in individual composition, as to suggest that they stem from something beyond the high-school classroom. They suggest, as closer examination can illustrate, that the free-association method was opening to view evidence of very particular cultural imprinting independent of whatever degree of sophistication the students had encountered in high school. To explore the nature and content of this particularity, we need to examine this ad-hoc pantheon more closely.

At first glance, it is the uniformity that is the most striking. In fact, given the absence of the focusing presence of Lincoln, Washington, and Jefferson, the similarity of the lists is really astonishing. To repeat the previous analysis, we find here that only nineteen different names appear in the "top ten" for the seven years, out of the seventy possible, for a Diversity Index of .15—not as low as for Question One, but still strikingly diminutive.

Three of the top ten are the same in all seven years: Betsy Ross, the apocryphal creator of the first American flag; Paul Revere, the horsebacked bearer of the message of revolution; and John Smith, the leader of the first successful colonial settlement in Virginia. Another five rank in this grouping in at least five of the seven years: Columbus; Eli Whitney, inventor of both interchangeable parts and the cotton gin and hence the symbol of the rise of both northern industry and southern slave society; Meriwether Lewis and George Rogers Clark, explorers of the American West who are counted as one—they have become almost a fused individual in the memories of students, always listed together as "Lewis and Clark" or, in more than one instance, Lewis N. Clark; the frontiersman Daniel Boone; and Harriet Tubman, the heroic escaped slave who returned to lead others to freedom, whose presence is the one sign that a century-old pantheon has begun to respond to the recent sensitivity to the centrality of blacks as agents of change, not merely objects of misfortune, in American history.

Table 2.3
Question Two: Seven Samples

1974	1976	1978	1982
1. B. Ross	1. B. Ross	1. B. Ross	1. B. Ross
2. P. Revere	2. P. Revere	2. E. Whitney	2. P. Revere
3. Columbus	3. Columbus	3. D. Boone	3. J. Smith
4. J. Smith	4. E. Whitney	4. P. Revere	4. T. Edison
5. Pocahontas	5. T. Paine	5. Pocahontas	5. E. Whitney
6. B. Arnold	6. H. Tubman	6. Columbus	6. D. Crockett
7. Lewis & Clark	7. J. Smith	7. Lewis & Clark	7. Columbus
8. D. Boone	8. Lewis & Clark	8. J. Smith	8. H. Tubman
9. E. Whitney	9. B. Arnold	9. R. Fulton	9. D. Boone
10. D. Crockett	10. D. Boone	10. T. Edison	10. F. S. Key
11. F. S. Key	11. Pocahontas	11. A. Hutchinson	11. N. Turner
12. T. Paine	12. F. S. Key	12. D. Crockett	12. F. Nightingale
13. J. P. Jones	13. J. Brown	13. F. Douglass	13. T. Paine
14. N. Hawthorne	14. J. P. Jones	14. C. McCormick	14. J. W. Booth
15. H. B. Stowe	15. Lafayette	15. N. Hawthorne	15. P. DeLeon
16. R. Williams	16. J. W. Booth	16. H. Tubman	16. Sitting Bull
17. M. Standish	17. D. Crockett	17. H. B. Stowe	17. M. Washington
18. G. W. Carver	18. R. Fulton	18. Balboa	18. E. Allen
	19. G. W. Carver	19. G. W. Carver	19. G. W. Carver

1983	1984	1985
1. B. Ross	1. B. Ross	1. B. Ross
2. P. Revere	2. P. Revere	2. P. Revere
3. Lewis & Clark	3. H. Tubman	3. H. Tubman
4. J. Smith	4. Lewis & Clark	4. Columbus
5. T. Edison	5. J. W. Booth	5. F. S. Key
6. J. W. Booth	6. D. Madison	6. J. Smith
7. H. Tubman	7. J. Smith	7. Pocahontas
8. E. Whitney	8. F. S. Key	8. Lewis & Clark
9. D. Boone	9. Pocahontas	9. E. Whitney
10. T. Paine	10. H. B. Stowe	10. B. Franklin
11. Pocahontas	11. D. Boone	11. J. W. Booth
12. M. Washington	12. T. Edison	12. T. Paine
13. Columbus	13. B. Franklin	13. M. Washington
14. B. Arnold	14. R. Fulton	14. C. Attucks
15. A. Burr	15. B. Arnold	15. J. Brown
16. F. Douglass	16. C. Barton	16. G. W. Carver
17. Sitting Bull	17. J. Brown	17. S. B. Anthony
18. J. Hancock	18. J. P. Jones	18. D. Boone
19. F. S. Key	19. A. G. Bell	19. N. Hale
20. G. W. Carver	20. G. W. Carver	20. M. Pitcher

Considering the entire list, in a total of 135 possibilities, only 44 different names are listed, and of these 13 appear in at least five of the seven years. Our Diversity Index for Question Two's full list is thus .21, only slightly higher than the .15 on Question One. The Consensus Indexes for Question Two are of course considerably lower than for the canonical list of Question One, unsurprising given that the second question prompts responses unconstrained by the familiar political pantheon. In fact, it is remarkable that they are as low as they are, given the infinite range of possible responses. In this respect, it is especially significant that the diversity and consensus in the top ten list for Question Two do not alter very much when the full range of responses is considered: indeed, by at least one measure (which in a last fit of social science I will call the Consensus Decay Index) there is more consistency between the top ten and the full list on Question Two (C.D.I. of 30) than on Question One (C.D.I. of 37). That is to say, on Question Two there is a slower increase than on Question One in the variation encountered as we move away from the most popular images at the top, which means more consistency in the images students have offered over the years in response to this question.

It is hard to know how much we can generalize from the uniformity of these lists, or how much interpretive weight they can bear. Perhaps all this is merely an artifact of my western New York sample, or the curriculum of the New York State's primary and secondary schools; I would be the first to concede that a similar survey in Waco, Texas, for example, would produce a somewhat different list. But I believe regional variation would be far less than expected, that the consistency of the lists—arguably more at the heart of their significance than the precise content—might well be as striking. This is because I think the free association producing the lists is tapping a very particular kind of cultural memory, one whose hold is general rather than a product of particular associations. Buffalo is a heavily ethnic city, for example, and many of our students come from a highly self-conscious Polish-American community. Thaddeus Kosciuszko is paraded every year and is certainly well known to these students—yet he has rarely been mentioned on any list *at all*, nor do the tallies suggest much imprint of any other ethnic identification.

There is some more positive and empirical support for my claim of generality in one carefully controlled replication of the survey in another locale. After learning of my experiment and discussing it in correspondence, the noted cultural geographer Wilbur Zelinsky tried it on a large group of his own students at Penn State—not terribly far from Buffalo, but not an identical culture area either, and one whose students are shaped by a different precollege curriculum. Even with the accumulating weight of my own evidence, we were both astounded by the uniformity of the results in Pennsylvania: on Questions One and Two alike, thirteen of the top fifteen names were identical to those on my Buffalo surveys, in nearly identical rank order, headed once again by the unsinkable Betsy Ross. The tiny differences in the lists almost disappeared in the fuller list of twenty or so: William Penn turns out to be the only figure unique to Pennsylvania rankings. Zelinsky's lists even reproduce some of the peculiarities of mine, such as the curiously misplaced presence of George Washington Carver and Thomas Edison, who belong in a different time period, and the Americanization of Florence Nightingale, who belongs on another continent.

In addition, Zelinsky added one methodological flourish whose products bear quite usefully on the broader issues I raised earlier: he asked his students whether they had ever taken a college American history course before (roughly 30 percent had, and 70 percent had not). Given the cultural importance many attach to exposure to history courses in the curriculum, it is interesting to ask what changes when Zelinsky's responses are tallied under these headings.

The answer is, absolutely nothing; the lists compiled by history and nonhistory students are virtually identical in composition and even rank order. Some individual names obtain slightly higher support from history students (Samuel Adams and Jeff Davis on Question One, Davy Crockett and John Wilkes Booth on Question Two) while others gain proportionally more of their votes from nonhistory students (George Washington Carver and William Penn). But the breakdown of support for most of the names shows only the most modest divergence from the 30/70 breakdown of the class as a whole. There is a final poetic justice in the fact that the one figure on Question Two at absolute dead center, listed in absolutely identical proportions by history and nonhistory students alike, is none other than Betsy Ross. Whatever students may or may not have learned in college history courses (and, as I shall argue, high-school history courses as well) seems to have little to do with the images drawn forth by this exercise.[4]

Having mollified the gods of empiricism, let us turn to the task of explaining in broader cultural terms the patterns we have uncovered. Each list profiles a strikingly consistent pantheon of generally received and recalled cultural heroes, legends, and near-mythic figures. Quite apparently, we are examining here evidence of cultural transmission, perhaps as mediated through the primary schools and popular culture. Accordingly, my introductory lecture, from the first year, has had less to do with the high-school curricula I had expected to engage in battle, than with what I came to pose, for the students, as a kind of anthropological question: "If all you knew about American culture was what you could deduce from this list, what would you know?"

Thus viewed as a cultural artifact, the profile offered in each list is anything but random. Rather, it stands as a dramatic elaboration of what Catherine Albanese has termed the "presumption of newness" at the core of the American myth.[5] Indeed, what we see here is a broadening of this theme into an ongoing fixation on creation myths of origin and innovation.

In this, myth must be understood as the driving force behind history: John Smith and Pocahontas were real, of course, but manifestly it is the mythic scene in which the "love" of the Indian "princess" saves the explorer from a "savage" death that accounts for the high-ranking presence of both these figures in the imagination of my students. Such a mythic framework reaches out to the explorers, from Columbus to the Siamese-twin Lewis and Clark, who define the nation by "beginning" its history, their "discovery" of space really a beginning of America's historical time, again and again. It includes both the Revolutionary progenitors and the practical inventors like Eli Whitney who are remembered as initiators of America's distinctive epoch of technological time.

It is interesting, in this regard, to note the place of inventor Thomas Edison in fourteenth place on the Question Two tally, near the top, and the black botanist George Washington Carver as well, who brings up the rear almost every time, and who is the only figure never to appear in the top ten who nevertheless *also* ranks on the overall list in *every* one of the seven samples. (On Zelinsky's poll, he is the single figure most disproportionately listed by nonhistory students.)

As late-nineteenth/early-twentieth-century figures, both Edison and Carver represent an overriding of the instructions to focus on an earlier time period. It hardly seems coincidental, given contemporary anxiety about ungraspable technological change and uncontrollable corporate organization on a worldwide scale, that the *only* regularly repeated chronological "mistakes" are these comfortable symbols of practical genius and human-scale progress.

And for a white society shuttling between racial guilt and fear, the symbol of Carver has always offered an additional all-too-convenient balm. The myth of the patient experimenter, the "credit to his race" who discovered manifold new uses for the lowly peanut, has long obscured the reality of a man whose docile acquiescence to the racism of turn-of-the-twentieth-century America, in contrast to genuine black leaders like W. E. B. DuBois and even Booker T. Washington, may be said to have contributed more than his very modest accomplishments to a not-quite-natural selection for immortality in the evolution of American memory.

There is also something beyond coincidence in the recurrence of John Wilkes Booth and Benedict Arnold, who represent for an innocent nation the serpent-traitors whose evil also sets history in motion—necessary

preludes to the transcendent triumph of good. As these observations sug
gest, the list is not only composed of quasi-mythic figures: as a collectiv
portrait, it has a kind of mythic structure and completeness itself, a char
acter confirmed by its re-creation year after year in nearly identical terms.

But the most compelling indication of this character is the seemingl
unshakable hold of Betsy Ross on the first-place position, a truly phenom
enal record that cries out for explanation, as it has occasioned a good dea
of discussion in my classes each year. Even given everything said so far, i
is still not immediately apparent why this *particular* mythic figure ha
been discovered so much more frequently than others by the searchin
beam of free-association memory.

Part of the explanation may lie in a kind of psychological/feminist in
terpretation generated by one class discussion: the notion that the com
mand to produce names of those not in positions of public power led th
genderized imaginations of students through the following sequence: non
public means domestic and private, domestic and private means women
women means Betsy Ross. I think there may be something to this, thoug
it still begs a number of questions. The framework of civil religion an
comparative mythology provides some additional insights, however, an
all combined may serve to make the Betsy Ross hegemony less mystica
and more instructive.

The flag, of course, is the primary symbol of what is distinctive abou
the United States. It represents the core of our nationality—that politica
identity declared and constituted in the epochal revolutionary experienc
whose artifactual yet genuine religious content Albanese has documente
so powerfully. As Marshall Smelser has written, the flag "has assumed a
moral value transcending the mundane purposes of national identity. As a
tribal totem, it satisfies the real and almost universal hunger for a public
symbol of spiritual kinship above and invulnerable to the contentions and
changes of politics—and for which no other totem is available to the
United States."[6] If this is true, then there is nice logic to Betsy Ross's
predominant place in a structure of creation-myth figures and heroic
progenitors: she represents this most inclusive of symbols of national
identity, an identity perhaps more fragile and in need of shoring up
because of its uniquely political character than many other national
cultures.

The Ross hegemony also helps to bring that presidential list of Question One within the interpretation developed here, for its figures are also
more powerful as symbols of political cohesion and identity than as historical figures per se. Indeed, Washington himself "absorbed and unified the
elements from the classical and Christian past, becoming, for Americans, a
divine man."[7] Beyond helping us to respect, and thereby understand, a
sometimes ludicrous apotheosis that began even in Washington's lifetime,

Albanese's discussion provides a context for some final reflections on the essentially religious meaning of Betsy Ross's place in this collective portrait.

Albanese documents how the revolutionary sons made themselves into Fathers, with Washington the *primus inter pares*, literally the spiritual Father of the Nation. She also shows how his spiritual meaning came to obscure his real existence: his wife Martha faded from legendary image and, relatively speaking, from our memories, because "kindred as was the soul of the father of the country to his wife, it had proved to be far more closely interfused with the structures of meaning and values of his countrymen. Washington . . . had become a grand collective representative, a tribal totem." And in the process, fictive and symbolic kin came to replace his real family in popular imagination: thus the common celebration of Lafayette as the "beloved and adopted son."[8]

Albanese could go on further with the myth, but Betsy Ross's symbolic role allows us to complete the picture. To this end, it is important to note that the Betsy Ross story is a product of a later style of religio-mythic craftsmanship. The actual Betsy Ross had, demonstrably, no role whatsoever in the actual creation of any actual first flag. But more importantly, her story itself played no part in revolutionary-era tradition or mythmaking even at its most instrumental. In fact, the flag story emerged only a century later in Philadelphia, around the time of the centennial exposition of 1876. The reasons for this were prosaic, not to say mercenary; but as Albanese reminds us, however intentional and instrumental, such self-consciousness does not exclude deeper levels of cultural meaning and expression.[9]

It is hard to avoid the speculation that the latter-day invention of the mythic Betsy Ross—and her immediate public enshrinement—came as a kind of needed supplement to the revolutionary myth, a final step in the "humano-centric" articulation of essentially religious beliefs and experiences. If George is the Father of the Country—of the nation, of all the American sons and daughters—then surely Betsy Ross exists symbolically as the Mother, who gives birth to our collective symbol.

One can go further. If Washington is, indeed, God the Father, the iconography of Betsy Ross is unmistakable: she is the Blessed Virgin Mary of our civil religion. A plain woman is visited by a distant God, and commanded to be the vehicle, through their immaculate collaboration, of a divine creation. And indeed, in the classroom pageants enacted by generations of American schoolchildren over the past century, this is exactly what we see: Washington calls on the humble seamstress Betsy Ross in her tiny home and asks her if she will make the nation's flag to his design. And Betsy promptly brings forth—from her lap—the flag, the nation itself, and the promise of freedom and natural rights for all mankind.

There is a final note of confirmation for this hypothesis in the rathe after-the-fact addition of Betsy Ross to our national mythology. For th cult of the Virgin Mother itself was a rather late development in Christia theology, a medieval elaboration of an undeveloped dimension of th gospels, a statement, perhaps, that for a fully satisfying religious symbolism Sons and Fathers were not quite enough. If this interpretation seem excessive for dealing with what are, after all, only a series of trite relics fron grade-school primers, then I ask you to remember Catherine Albanese' caution that the contrivance or superficiality of myth-making does no necessarily deny, and may even tend to confirm, its deeper cultura functions.

This observation provides a good pivot on which to return to the ques tions with which we began—the relevance of this exploration in historica trivia for the august debates on history and education that loom so large i contemporary discussion.

On one level, my results can be read as a confirmation of the diagnosis that something is seriously wrong if college students cannot come up with lists showing more depth and grasp than these; if college courses—as Zelinsky's data suggest—or even high-school courses, as the overal survey demonstrates—have so little impact, then surely we are in some kind of trouble. The almost childish character of the revealed pantheon seems quite consistent with the diagnosis that we are producing generations for whom a meaningful national history in even some of its richness and complexity is simply not an accessible resource. And as such the survey can only reinforce the resonance many history teachers must feel when they encounter the documented ignorance that so exercises William J. Bennett, Diane Ravitch, Lynne Cheney, et al. Everyone who teaches history must have his or her own horror story that seems to confirm the ominous collapse of rope bridges across the generation gap.[10]

As I have argued, however, the surveys are more interesting when taken as evidence of what students do know, rather than what they don't. If the results say little one way or the other about how much history these students actually may know, they are evidence that cultural imagery seems to be reproduced in our young people with startling consistency and regularity. And this conclusion casts something of a shadow over the current jeremiads, whose core concerns, I would argue, are at bottom more fundamentally cultural and political than educational. This point is worth at least brief examination by way of conclusion.

The sermons being preached in this crusade are difficult to deal with as texts, because they slide so fluidly along a spectrum of analysis ranging from the high-minded and humanistic to the vulgarly political and instrumental. At the former end, we find the calls for exposure to the complexity of historical studies, for the cultivation of the critical mind, and for provision of the basic orientation to the real world and its history that any citizen will need to understand the present and make intelligent choices in the future. It is hard to see how anyone could fail to be shocked by the documentation effects on students of an almost willful indifference to the value of historical consciousness and training, and the effects on teachers, especially in the secondary schools, of decades of overemphasis on pseudo-professional training programs and methods at the expense of subject and substance.

It is a different matter when these unexceptionable themes are given a more particular emphasis: that students need not just more of History, but rather more of "our" national history. To a degree, the argument still holds: citizenship in a democracy requires the critical skills that such training should provide, and a certain core orientation in the history and geography of one's country is arguably essential to knowing what the society is all about. But in most formulations, the educational critique is sufficiently expansive to suggest a different animus behind it: the problem is that our students are spending too much time on "them"—the rest of the world, global and comparative studies, and so forth—rather than on the "us" at home. And to the extent they do study "us," it is the wrong us—too much emphasis on social history, minorities, women, and the like, rather than on the political and military core of national tradition.

This is held problematic, both symptom and cause of a fragmented national unity, cohesion, and will in the face of grave political, economic, and military threats from without, and even from within. Virtually every one of the core documents slips into this mood sooner rather than later, after the appropriate genuflections at the altar of humanism and the critical spirit. The issue is put starkly in terms of American competitiveness, the Cold War, and the danger of ethnic and linguistic pluralism run rampant.

Since I haven't the time to demonstrate this point by citing chapter and verse from the new scriptures, let me offer a single picture. This lead page from a 1985 *New York Times Magazine* article by Diane Ravitch touches every base: the headline announces the problem in its most generalized form—the "Decline and Fall of Teaching History." The subhead slides into the Americanization of the cultural literacy problem, masking the shift of focus with syntax that raises concern about plain old literacy at the *Times*: "An ignorance or indifference about studying our past has become cause for concern." And finally, there is a picture, suspended between the two: a teacher leads a small group discussion in a global studies course that is, elsewhere in the article, an object of ridicule. Manifestly, the picture is intended to illustrate both "Decline and Fall" and "Ignorance and Indifference." Yet the class seems lively and intense; the lesson plan on the blackboard behind the teacher carries the outline for what could be a satisfying history lecture in any college course. What, then, is the picture

New York Times Magazine, 17 November 1985, p. 50
Courtesy Jeanne Strongin © 1987 and The New York Times Company © 1985.

doing here? Could it have anything to do with the fact that the teacher is black, the students black and perhaps Hispanic, and the lesson plan involves Russian history on the eve of the Revolution?[11]

I submit that this captures perfectly the tension between the explicit text, couched in broadly acceptable abstract terms about history, and the deeply political subtext of the current educational crusade. Beneath the huffing and puffing about historical studies lies a fear not dissimilar to that propelling the "Americanization" efforts that so dominated education and politics in the United States in the early years of the twentieth century, fueled by a terror of immigrant cultures and concern for the future of the Anglo-Saxon race and heritage. It is fascinating how often, in the current litany, these educational efforts are taken to represent a kind of golden age to which we should return.

If all this has a quaint ring so soon after the Statue of Liberty Centennial, the explicit Cold War fixation strikes a much more ominous tone: William J. Bennett explicitly grounded his own critique of the schools, for example, on the proposition that they have embraced the doctrine of, in Jeane Kirkpatrick's term, "moral equivalence," willfully offering education "designed to prevent future generations of American intellectuals from telling the difference between the U.S. and the U.S.S.R."[12]

In all this, then, concern for education has been redefined in highly ideological terms: the point of education is not individual but national; the object of improvement in training in history is the production of obedient, patriotic citizens who share a set of presumptions about the United States, its people, economy, and relation to the other peoples of the world. The argument has travelled a long way from its humanistic origins, arriving at the point where education and cultural/political indoctrination seem almost indistinguishable.

Indeed, in one of the more remarkable documents in the current literature, they *are* indistinguishable. Sidney Hook's 1984 lecture "Education in Defense of a Free Society" is a kind of Ur-text of the cultural literacy movement, outlining a set of themes that reappear again and again, less baldly, in the writings and speeches of Bennett, Ravitch, Cheney, et al. To Hook, the issue is "whether we possess the basic social cohesion and solidarity today to survive the challenge to our society . . . posed by the global expansion of communism"; the role of the schools—primary and secondary especially—is to generate sufficient loyalty through what he freely acknowledges is an embrace of propaganda and indoctrination (critical thought comes later, he says); and in the final analysis "no institutional changes of themselves will develop that bond of community needed to sustain our nation in times of crisis without a prolonged schooling in the history of our free society, its martyrology, and its national tradition."[13]

Hook's explicit reference to martyrology, tradition, and the need for cultural indoctrination in the primary and secondary schools brings us back to Betsy Ross and the tables of data I have been discussing here. For Hook, Bennett, Cheney, Ravitch, and others in what William Greider has called the "Bloom and Doom" school, we are in trouble on every front: the crisis of historical amnesia at the higher levels, the decline of formal studies in history, and the deterioration of critical thinking are taken to be linked to a presumed corrosion of national spirit and will, evidenced in a declining respect for and awareness of the binding symbols of national tradition at the most basic levels. To such critics, there is no contradiction in calling for patriotic indoctrination under the umbrella of a culturally binding nationalism, on the one hand, and intellectually challenging studies in history, on the other. The assumption is that a shared cultural memory and historical consciousness ought to be close to the same thing, or at least linked in some developmental or cumulative sense.[14]

The evidence I have presented suggests that this philosophically dubious proposition is also without foundation empirically. There is no indication in my data that the deeper chords of cultural memory, in terms of the hold of national historical symbols, have weakened in the slightest while a deeper grasp of history is evidently slipping away—in fact, as I have shown, the consistency and extraordinary uniformity in the images offered up by students indicates that the "Bloom and Doom" school and their followers have little cause for concern: the structure of myth and heroes, martyrs and mothers, is firmly in place.

This does not mean there is no crisis in the teaching of history, no deficiency in the historical consciousness with which our young people perceive the swiftly changing world around them. It does suggest, however, that frantic injections of cultural symbolism will not be the solution to the epidemic, and that in fact indoctrination and education need, if anything, to be more effectively decoupled. Finally, it suggests what most history teachers already know: that alienated students cannot be bullied into attention or retention; that authoritarian cultural intimidation is likely to be met by a further and more rapid retreat; and that there may well be, in that alienation itself, statements about the claims of the present on the past worth our respect, attention, and response.

I have concluded in my own teaching that the evidently massive, uniform subsurface reefs of cultural memory are part of the problem, not resources for a solution. As such, however, they merit immense respect from pedagogic navigators. My ongoing experiment in the survey course has convinced me that we need to realize what we are up against, in our classrooms and in political life more broadly. We must understand the depth of the cultural symbolism our students and fellow citizens carry inside them long before entering our classrooms, if ever they do. Appreciating how our historical imagination is held in the powerful grip of cultural memory becomes a necessary first step if we are to discover and teach other approaches to understanding historical processes and reality. If not quite "historians against history," than we must all become at least history teachers against history, in a more profound and complex sense than many of us have assumed.

Notes

1. The best sellers, of course, are E. D. Hirsch, Jr., *Cultural Literacy: What Every American Needs to Know* (Boston: Houghton Mifflin, 1987) and Allan Bloom, *The Closing of the American Mind: How Higher Education Has Failed Democracy and Impoverished the Souls of Today's Students* (New York: Simon and Schuster, 1987). The 1987 NEH study by chairman Lynne Cheney is *American Memory: A Report on the Humanities in the Nation's Public Schools*, which follows the 1983 report of the National Commission on Excellence in Education, *A Nation at Risk: The Imperative for Educational Reform*. Both are available from the Government Printing Office. The newer study is Diane Ravitch and Chester E. Finn, Jr., *What Do Our 17-Year-Olds Know?* (New York: Harper & Row, 1987). For a representative example of the mass-mediated digestion of this debate, see the cover story on "Cultural Illiteracy," *U.S. News and World Report*, 28 September 1987.

2. See two useful reviews of the Ravitch/Finn study that develop this point: Deborah Meier and Florence Miller, "The Book of Lists," and Etta Moser, "What They *Do* Know," both in the *Nation*, 9 January 1988.

3. The best single discussion of this approach, as well as the best case study application, is Catherine L. Albanese, *Sons of the Fathers: The Civil Religion of the American Revolution* (Philadelphia: Temple University Press, 1976).

4. I much appreciate Professor Zelinsky's interest in the problem and his sending me the data from his 1 March 1984 survey of a Geography 1 class of 115 students. This material is discussed and presented with his kind permission (Letter to author, 5 March 1984).

5. Albanese, *Sons of the Fathers*, 9, 28.

6. Ibid., 261.

7. Ibid.,158-59.

8. Ibid., 172.

9. See the full and interesting account in the *Encyclopedia of Philadelphia*, 1054-55.

10. My personal favorite is Professor Manning Marable's report of the black student in a black studies class who came up to ask, "Now, who is this Malcolm the Tenth they mention in this book, and what was he king of, anyway?" This is instructive in indicating that the problem of cultural loss, whatever else it may mean, is

a shared one, not simply a matter, as usually presented, of the dominant culture's heritage being insufficiently respected by those held to be in need of its ministrations.

11. Diane Ravitch, "Decline and Fall of Teaching History," *New York Times Magazine*, 17 November 1985, 50f.

12. Quoted in Walter Goodman, "Conservatives' Theme: The West is Different," *New York Times*, 5 May 1985, a report of an anticommunism conference, the first event sponsored by the State Department's new and controversial Office for Public Diplomacy.

13. Sidney Hook, "Education in Defense of a Free Society," *Commentary*, July 1984. The speech was delivered on the occasion of Hook's receiving the Jefferson award, bestowed as its highest honor by NEH, for "intellectual achievement in the humanities."

14. The reference is to a witting review of Bloom's polemic: William Greider, "Bloom and Doom," *Rolling Stone*, 8 October 1987. For other relevant critiques, see Martha Nussbaum, "Undemocratic Vistas," *New York Review of Books*, 5 November 1987, and Robert Pattison, "On the Finn Syndrome and the Shakespeare Paradox," *Nation*, 30 May 1987.

COMMENT

Kenneth Foote*, a cultural geographer at The University of Texas at Austin, expands Michael H. Frisch's discussion of cultural memory as reflected in history education to include cultural memory as seen in the American landscape.*

I think it is no coincidence that I, as a geographer, have been asked to comment upon Michael Frisch's paper. Geography and history have long been regarded as parallel disciplines and my particular research, as a historical geographer and landscape historian, concerns the way the American landscape has been shaped to reflect a collective and selective view of the past. Further, I am interested in how the act of shaping the landscape has itself assisted Americans in their myth making and tradition building. At the moment, my primary interest lies in what might be termed America's "landscape of violence," the way Americans have come to celebrate some episodes of tragedy and violence as part of the national past, while choosing to overlook and even efface others. Violence seems to expose for study relationships which are of interest to scholars of memory, history, and representations of the collective past. The only point I would make as a geographer about these representations is that they are not solely cognitive or oral, but can become fixed—almost cosmographical—in landscape through the use of monuments, memorials, and markers. In Texas, for example, a person can gain an appreciation for the shaping of these sacred places by visiting the Alamo, Goliad, and San Jacinto battlefields, and even the John F. Kennedy cenotaph in Dallas.

In addressing these issues from a different perspective, Frisch is posing a question about the content of American collective memory, in particular the stability of this content and its means of propagation. More importantly, he sets his discussion in the context of current debate about historical and cultural literacy. The value of the paper is, then, that it tries to expose empirically the content of the somewhat illusory concept of collective memory and uses this information to enter a popular debate which is sorely in need of factual grounding. In stressing this point, I think we need not belabor the paper's method. Frisch is very careful to qualify his tallies and indices and maintains, from the start, that his findings are suggestive rather than definitive. Certainly, I would leave it to Loftus to critique the form of the questions and address the suggestibility of the students. It is rather more important to underline what I see as the real strength of the paper: Frisch rejects a decidedly pessimistic, but now commonplace, appraisal of what students don't know in favor of asking what they do know about American history. By turning the tables on recent critics of education, Frisch is able to offer two fascinating insights: (1) American college students are not as historically illiterate as they are portrayed; and (2) there is a surprising consistency and stability to what they do know about the American past.

I, too, come from a discipline where scholars begin to foam in contemplation of geographical, not historical, illiteracy. And I daresay there is some substance to their concern. But again, the questions asked about this illiteracy tend to generate their own self-serving and predetermined answers. If I asked my students in Austin to locate Waco on a blank outline map of Texas, only a minority would succeed. But if I asked for directions from Austin to Waco, most would point me north on I-35 and tell me to drive for two hours, just as they could tell me the results of any recent athletic event between the Baylor Bears and the Texas Longhorns. The problem is that I-35, the Bears, and the Longhorns aren't—as E. D. Hirsch would have it—among what every American "needs to know." Of course, Hirsch isn't a Texan. But isn't it the case, as Frisch seems to say, that Hirsch is asking the wrong questions?

Perhaps the answer lies in considering what geographical illiteracy implies. Certainly it isn't that students are likely to get lost. At spring break, campuses throughout the country clear as students head for Taos, Aspen,

Padre Island, and other points west and south. And the roads are not li
tered with lost motorists in stranded Camaros. Geographical illiterac
implies, instead, that people lack the knowledge to make well-formed de
cisions about the world and their place in it. Unfortunately, this criterio
cannot be transferred, without modification, to the discussion of historica
illiteracy. We hope that knowledge of the past will inform our decisions
but the problem is that our interpretation of the past seems to change t
meet the demands of contemporary life. As many historians have pointe
out, including Frisch in some of his earlier writings, "historical under
standings change and grow in the process of being carried across intellec
tual generations."[1] Perhaps what we are seeing, then, in the curren
cultural literacy debate is simply one generation criticizing the new his
torical reality of a younger generation.

Historical knowledge as measured by so-called facts—as arrayed i
Frisch's pantheon of important Americans—is unreliable in that it fails t
tell us how this information will be used to form judgments which wi
shape contemporary life. Periodic debate about the intent of the framers o
the U.S. Constitution demonstrates how selective can be the reading o
historical text and context. The issue then, as regards Frisch's hall of fame
is how his students will employ their knowledge to make sense of a
changing world. In effect, how will they use their collective memory to
face fresh perceptions of contemporary events? Perhaps I can best reinforce this point by recalling the closing scene of the movie *Platoon*. As the
film's hero, Chris Taylor, flies from the carnage he has witnessed in
Vietnam, he says: "Those of us who did make it have an obligation to build
again, to teach to others what we know, and to try—with what's left of our
lives—to find a goodness and meaning to this life." The beauty—or the
horror—of the observation lies in its ambiguity about war in general and
Vietnam in particular. Some viewers may hear in Taylor's message a call to
pacifism, others a call to fight only those wars which are morally
unequivocal. The movie is hedging its assessment of the Vietnam War, but
so too have many Americans over the past fifteen years. As to the meaning
of Vietnam, and so many events of the national past, you, the viewer, are
left to decide.

Notes

1. Michael H. Frisch and Daniel J. Walkowitz, eds., *Working-Class America: Essays on Labor, Community, and American Society* (Urbana: University of Illinois Press, 1983).

DIALOGUE I

The following discussion among Paul Thompson, Elizabeth F. Loftus, Michael . Frisch, and psychologist Sally Browder is based on the preceding essays.

LIZABETH F. LOFTUS: I found very intriguing Glenace Edwall's dis-ussion about the cathartic value of telling one's story, and how the value iat has for the respondent gives a certain power to the interviewer. I was oping that Paul could tell us whether he agrees or disagrees, whether it ts in his experiences. I've never thought about it from the point of view f the kind of interviews I do.

AUL THOMPSON: I'm not sure whether *power* is the word which I vould use. I am sure that is right; the power exists. The point that Edwall lso suggested, the power of the interview experience, I certainly agree vith completely. In fact, in England there has been enormous development f reminiscence therapy, which is based on that particular power of atharsis—very impressively. For instance, oral history is being used to ielp old people who are confused or mute or whatever by stimulating nemory to get them talking and to recover something of their life spirits nd their sense of self. This is interesting because it is almost the reverse of vhat Elizabeth Loftus does in her work in courtrooms with eyewitness estimony. I am sure there is a power which the interviewer can assume, ut I have never experienced the feeling that it was a kind of malevolent ower that you could abuse.

I always felt that it was marvelous if you realized that somebody had een helped by telling their story. You don't always know that at the time. t is something that comes back to you just occasionally, something that ou are told. The first time I heard that was very early on in my oral history vork with one of the first people I ever recorded. He didn't say anything o me himself, but when I went back to see him the next year, he had died, ind his daughter told me that our interview had just transformed the last nonths of his life. He had just been waiting for me to come again. It had iever occurred to me that this was possible, and that was what started me hinking about it.

MICHAEL H. FRISCH: The point has implications on any number of levels, from the higher intellectual and political ones to the simple guide-book level, but Paul's point is really well taken: it is very important to be aware of the power of oral history. Sometimes it may be just another in-terview to you, but it is a very major element in the interviewee's life, or it

comes at a point where the interviewee has literally given somethi
important of himself or herself. Either the thank-you note or the telepho
call after the interview or the various ways in which an intervie
relationship is respected is a very important aspect of the work involved
the oral history process. When you are doing fifty interviews for a projec
it is often easy to overlook it, but I think those responses are, in a ve
practical sense, ways in which respect for the oral history situation can b
addressed, and they should be cultivated.

It is a complicated relationship on both sides of the microphon
Whether it is a struggle for power or simply a kind of moral power th
people on each side have, it is helpful to realize that the power is there *o*
both sides. People are not just raw data that we are encountering for
given project.

THOMPSON: It seemed to me that Beth Loftus's very fascinating expe
iments were dealing with the kind of memory which we regard, as or
historians, as unreliable: the memory of fleeting incidents. Beth, could yo
recommend to us the sort of experiment that perhaps we oral historian
should be carrying out—if we were able to—to discover the role of sug
gestibility and potential for errors in more reliable memory, such as ar
found in repeated patterns of everyday life in childhood or early work ex
perience or other memories which seem to be strongly reliable? Can yo
think of ways in which you could use your method to test that reliability?

LOFTUS: I am not sure whether my methods would work, at least for th
specific examples that you gave, because we are interested in episodi
memory as distinguished from semantic memory. Semantic memory in
volves the kind of memory that might be involved in repeated episodes o
knowledge, such as when you were in high school or when you worke
here for a period of years or whatever. One reason why the memories that
study are so malleable is because they refer to a specific event that occurred on a particular day at the particular time and only one time—no
repeatedly. I don't know whether the discoveries about these episodic
memories would apply to repeated memories. There are some other distortions that occur, though, that might. For example, other psychologists
have found that there is another distortion in memory that occurs regularly,
which is a prestige-enhancing shift. For example, people remember tha
they gave more money to charity than they really did; they took more
airplane trips than they really did. Now, these examples are getting close to
the repeated events that you are referring to. The finding here is that your
own thoughts and inferences as to the way you want to remember
yourself—in the absence of any specific external input, such as a suggestive or misleading question—can distort memory. I wouldn't be surprised
to find those kinds of distortions in memories of repeated events if the situation included a social desirability component.

FRISCH: This example would be a very crude approximation of some of the very interesting things Elizabeth is talking about. Let's say you had a group of people who had been involved in some controversial events in a labor union twenty or thirty years ago. They all had a similar involvement in the leadership of the union. You had one group of them interviewed by an interviewer who in various ways communicated the sense that, after all, all of that militancy was really childish, an embarrassment, and something which in mature society has been outgrown. Another interviewer communicated to his interviewees a desire to be somehow invigorated by contact with the heroic labor militancy of the past. You might find that the way in which people told their stories to those two interviewers differed—or maybe it would not differ. That might be an interesting way to test some of these questions.

The thing that you would be testing, and it's the thing I was most struck with in Elizabeth's talk, goes back to that question of power. In the interview relationship, there is the imposition of the power of the interrogator, that sense that somehow the interrogator is in touch with the appropriate framework, balanced against the degree to which the subject wants to please or at least be respectable within that framework. For example, if the interrogator uses the definite article with, say, a stop sign, implying that there definitely was a stop sign at the scene of an accident, then the person might say, "Well, I guess there must have been *the* stop sign there because who am I to doubt this person who is sitting there?" whether that person is representing an insurance company or a social-science enterprise or whatever. There are similar aspects in the oral history situation, particularly in interviewing people across a considerable social or class gap, where the nature of the interchange affects the responses. You could conceivably set up an artificial situation where you would send very different cues as to what it was okay to feel positive about in the past and you might find that would affect the results.

SALLY BROWDER: In many cases oral history interviews pertain to specific historic events which evoke episodic memories, not just semantic. The question then arises, can you trust those oral sources to relate accurately what happened, not just in the events of daily life, not just in looking at how a family went about tasks in a daily routine that was repeated numerous times but also in their involvement in a specific situation? When the event is a single event—whether you are a historian interviewing people who participated in that event or a psychologist interested in eyewitness testimony—the reliability of oral sources is still the issue.

THOMPSON: Well, as far as I'm concerned, an individual event is an extreme case where all the sources have to be treated with great skepticism. It has been shown again and again that, for instance, people will give accounts of events that they were not at, and they will displace information from one event to another, and so on. If you want to use oral sources for events, you have to use the method of triangulation sources—the written documents, several eyewitness accounts, and all tl positive reinforcements of memory you possibly can obtain. Even the you should be skeptical about it. I would take the view that certain oth kinds of memory are so much more central to people's sense of being th they might very well fall into the category of cases in which suggestic could *not* displace the memory. For instance, I don't believe that you ca actually suggest to somebody that they did completely different jobs fro what they did. I think it would be very interesting if we could work o how much of memory is as secure as that and where the boundaries are.

LOFTUS: That is exactly what I've been trying to do. I've been trying find out the conditions under which people are resistant to having the memories changed and the conditions under which they are particularl susceptible. I have shown that if you try to do something very blatan where they can clearly see a conflict between what is immediately avai able in their memory and what is being presented to them, they are goin to resist that information. The whole process of distorting memory has t be done subtly. Many of the questions in my experiments were very cleve questions in that I had the respondent's attention focused off of what was trying to do. "Did another car pass the red Datsun while it wa stopped at the stop sign?" You think this is a question about the car pass ing, and while you are concentrating on that, I am slipping a bit of infor mation into your memory. It is almost as if we are susceptible to thes things because we don't detect them at the time they are happening. But i the attempt at distortion is blatant, it is not going to work. If the source o the information is known to be biased and to want to deliberately mislea you for their own purposes, you are going to resist it.

There are few other variables that we have learned about that let u know that we are not completely, blindly affected by these things. In m own work I find it very difficult to discern individual difference variable that reliably predict who will be resistant and who will be susceptible t memory contamination. I can't say, for example, that intelligent people ar necessarily more resistant. There just doesn't seem to be very powerfu individual-difference variables. I think that given the right conditions, w are all susceptible to these kinds of distortions.

FRISCH: The really interesting things in the research are to explore the *processes* by which the distortions occur, which is rather different than simply saying they do occur. Loftus's more recent work seems to be doing that. I think the possibility of linking that work to oral history may be that memory distortion follows along a kind of spectrum. It may be caused by other things in the interview relationship. It may be the voice; it may be the gender of the interviewer which affects how memories are recalled and related. You could do a controlled experiment. Does having a male interviewer put questions to female respondents produce different levels of

ternalized error than having a female interrogator put questions to male
spondents? and so forth. It may have to do with questions of authority.
oes it matter whether it is somebody with a white coat representing a
boratory or somebody who is in a man-on-the-street situation such as a
levision reporter? There are a whole lot of questions about relationships
interviews, and I think we have analogies in oral history. I would agree
ith Elizabeth that it is a complex matter, not a straightforward one.

I always have to tell my students not to be too self-conscious. Most
eople go into their first interviews thinking, My god, if I ask the slightest
uestion wrong, it's going to destroy the source. They'll never say another
ord; they won't want to talk to me; the interview will collapse into since, and so forth. Yet what you often find when you look at a long tran-
cript is that it may be that the question that you insert completely throws
e person off or onto a track where they are accommodating you out of
oliteness, but it is not really their chosen subject matter. You ask them
bout something, they will respond, but then they will bring it back to
hat they want to talk about.

In one interview I was working with recently, if you did the equivalent
f stepping back ten feet, you could see the track of that interview. There
ay have been a lot of little zigs and zags, but when you looked at it from
distance, it was like an arrow. The interview as a whole was clearly what
hat person wanted to talk about in terms of their experience. And I had no
ffect on that. I'd pull them this way, I'd pull them that way, by kind of
oolishly asking a question that may or may not pertain, and they would
eal with it. But then they would come back more or less to what they
vanted to talk about. The conclusion I came to is reassuring in a way,
vhich is that it is a more alive relationship on both sides, that people have
heir ways of resisting our contamination to a certain extent. There is
robably a vast area in the center where it is up for grabs, who is in control
f the memory and what is happening to it.

A lot of contemporary history is a kind of feverish cultural war to fix
he story of the sixties or the seventies. *Newsweek* can hardly keep up
vith it; they are always labeling decades and trends and so forth. And if
ou ask what a lot of that is about, it is about putting a frame around the
tory. I think it has a lot to do with controlling the shape we give to a very
omplicated experience before it recedes too far into the past. You could
rgue that, on that level, that shaping needs to happen while it is still fresh
n peoples' minds. The same thing is happening with the recent Vietnam
novies, where that experience is still problematic enough, really subversive
nough, that the issue of how to frame it, how to get it within a story frame,
how to encapsulate it in memory becomes a very real and pressing concern
for many people.

BROWDER: Would you say that the need to frame experience is the cat-
alyst then for that sort of collective memory?

FRISCH: I don't know. Certainly it seems to me that in this society there are broader cultural politics, which perhaps are media driven but not necessarily, that really have become quite accelerated in modern times. These cultural politics seem to involve struggles over the basic form the complex experience has, almost wanting to preside over a story's passage into history. I mean, the sixties were no sooner cold in their calendar grave than the battle began over what form they would take.

LOFTUS: In an actual courtroom situation, where all eyes are upon you there are certain rules which guide the interview, what kinds of questions you can ask. For example, on direct examination, except under certain circumstances, you are not allowed to ask leading questions. Well, I'm not sure it would matter anyhow because by the time the witness has gotten to the courtroom, usually they are very well rehearsed on the critical facts. So it is not the prosecutors and the defense attorneys that you need to worry about asking the leading questions that might somehow distort the witness's memories. It is the police who are doing the initial interviews at the police station, where no tape recorders or videotape machines are recording it, and where the police have some sort of hypothesis about who did it or what happened or who pulled the knife first. They can communicate that hypothesis quite readily to the witnesses that they are interviewing just as, I suppose, an oral historian who has a hypothesis about whether something happened from the newspapers can communicate that hypothesis to a witness. So I'm not sure we have to worry about the courtroom situation so much, where we have reporters and judges and everybody watching for leading questions.

Now, you can still worry about the courtroom, not so much for distorting the witness's memory but for influencing the creation of the event in the mind of these jurors who, by definition, did not witness that event. So whether the lawyer refers to the event as a *smash* or *hit* or whether the lawyer refers to it as a *fight* or *struggle* or an *incident* could affect the way a juror mentally constructs the event. In that way, these references possibly could have a significant effect on the outcome of the trial.

FRISCH: The comment about the police station confessions is interesting because one of the frequent complexities arising from that situation are confessions whose validity is dubious. In a number of instances that I have studied in a different context, examples of what Elizabeth was talking about show up in the kind of confession extracted by force, and then there is another kind, where the confession is the result of psychological pressure, exhaustion, or guilt. There is a confession given, and yet it is not true. People internalize; they literally confess to things they did not do.

In Buffalo we are involved with a prison program, and there is a man there who is serving a life sentence for arson, an arson in which his wife and children were killed. In fact, the evidence seems fairly clear that no arson was committed, that it was just a fire. At the time of the fire, however, e man had the misfortune to be on bad terms with his wife, and he was ith another woman. The police came to him, announced that his wife and ildren were dead in the fire and that he was under arrest. In his collapse f grief, his own guilt at feeling that he had betrayed his wife, that he was n some level responsible, he confessed during a forty-eight-hour terrogation. He was convicted on the basis of that confession despite ny evidence that an arson was even committed. There is now excellent vidence that it was an electrical fire very similar to any other electrical fire. he trial was a catastrophe on many levels, but the root fact was that in at "oral history" exchange, through a variety of suggestions, he literally ternalized the other version of events. And, as he now would say, he ally did believe at the time he signed that confession that he had caused at fire. Then "caused that fire" became "set the fire," and for at least at week or two that he was in custody, he believed that he had set a fire, elieved everything they told him, signed the confession and believed it.

OFTUS: That is a very interesting story. I have a related confession tory. I once appeared on television with a man who had been on death ow in Florida for three years for a murder that he did not commit. He was sked, "What did you think about those years you were sitting on death ow knowing you didn't commit this murder?" And he said, "I started to hink maybe I did it. The police said I did it. The jury said I did it. The ewspapers said I did it. The judge said I did it. And I thought to myself, naybe I actually did it." To me, this was the ultimate success of postevent nformation to contaminate somebody's memory.

THOMPSON: We have been talking about the influence on a person's nemory of extremely traumatic events, including being put in prison, but here is just no way that you can compare the humble oral historian with he power of the police and the judiciary. The trouble is that, through ourtroom trials and psychological experiments, people have demonstrated very convincingly the ways in which memory is unstable. It is then assumed that almost nothing that we have in memory is in the least bit reliable. The fact is that memory is quite varied, and one of the first things you have to do as an oral historian is try to distinguish between different kinds of memory, different contexts for remembering, different subjects, and so on. What we need to learn to do is to realize that some kinds of memory are less reliable and that other kinds of memory are more reliable, and to start using some of the more positive supports for memory, the ways in which we can make it easier for somebody to remember reliably.

There are often factors, too, which make a difference. For example, we have learned that long-term memory does not necessarily sharpen as people get older. It is more that there comes a stage in life when people want to tell their story. In fact, that doesn't necessarily occur just when they are old. You get the same phenomenon, called "life review," with traumatic events. When people get divorced or widowed or retired, they very often want to talk and talk and talk about their lives. There comes point in life when people just really feel that they've not much to lose telling about their story, and they're less worried about what they say. Th memory may have, in fact, become less focused, but it's easier to get the to talk about it.

As people get older their are often problems of communication—hea ing loss, health problems, illness, and so on. On the other hand, with peop in middle life there are other kinds of problems, such as being so busy th it is very difficult to get them to find the time to reflect on their lives, ar that makes a tremendous difference. We found in our most recent work, fo instance, that it is almost impossible to get interviews with people wh have a whole series of burdens, such as, for instance, the woman who working full time and looking after her own household plus some agin parents. Not being able to get that kind of person to give an intervie unbalances the kind of representation that you have in oral history, an that has to do with the age cycle, definitely.

FRISCH: We need to watch out for the assumption that there is a kind normal interview relationship, which is unproblematic, which needs n reflection. What does it matter that somebody is a child or somebody i elderly? In fact, every interview relationship is just that, a *relationship*, relationship which is worth some attention in terms of whether the peopl are comfortable with each other. Are they the same class position or eth nicity? Should whites interview blacks? Should blacks interview blacks? is not an "either-or" situation, but there will be slightly different inter views and slightly different effects with each combination, and the ora historian needs to be aware of that, and in some way try to control for it o adjust to it in a variety of ways.

In my experience at least, almost every interview situation is wort some inquiry in terms of what is really going on, in terms of how these tw people are relating to each other across the microphone and what doe that have to do with the kind of questions I ask them? I'm doing a projec now on steelworkers, and I have had to learn a reasonable amount abou the steel-making process, but if I come in with a lot of very detailed ques tions to demonstrate my knowledge, it really undercuts the interview al most from the start. If I start by saying, "Explain to me," and allow them to instruct me on what goes on and sometimes even ask a not-very-well informed question, the interview goes a lot better. I get much more of thei own authority over the work situation that they've performed for twent years. But again, you have to look at each situation and try to develop strategies accordingly.

PHOENIX AND CHIMERA: THE CHANGING FACE OF MEMORY

Marigold Linton

'idely known for her work on long-term memory and the process of forgetting in hich she herself was the subject, Marigold Linton is an experimental psychologist · Arizona State University who specializes in memory cognition. In addition to her xpertise in the field of memory she has maintained a longtime commitment to the sychology of education for the American Indian. In 1980 she helped set the legal recedent in Utah which allowed psychologists to address the adequacy of yewitness testimony in a court of law. Here Linton establishes the connection be-veen historians and cognitive psychologists as she lays out some of the common-lities in human memory processes and places memory into the social milieu in hich it operates—how it is accessed, how it is affected by emotion, and how it hanges over time.

In considering this unique meeting between cognitive psychologists nd historians, I was irresistibly drawn to ask, "How are applied cognitive sychologists like oral historians?" I was intrigued by the similarities. We re more alike than I had thought.

We are brought together, of course, by our shared interest in memory. As a group," said John Neuenschwander in 1978, "oral historians have iore interest in and contact with human memory than any other profes-ionals except psychiatrists and psychologists. . . . Whenever they gather t professional meetings their shop talk invariably turns to anecdote swap-ing about strong, weak, and unique memories."[1] Neuenschwander, how-ver, regretted that "[Psychologists] prefer to study short-term memory nd have given scant attention to long-term reminiscence. Oral historians," e said, "encounter it all the time, but their uncritical interest has precluded ny serious study on their part. Thus the study of reminiscence as a factor f long-term memory has fallen beyond the reach of the psychologist and eneath the grasp of the oral historian."[2] Neuenschwander's concern eads to the next point of similarity.

Historians generally rely on written documents, a reliance that subtly estricts the range of credible sources. Oral historians argue that history is nriched by including evidence from a wider range of sources, in particular hose that are made possible by the use of oral narratives. Increasing the inds of acceptable sources permits the viewpoints of additional populations to be represented in histories. In an analogous way, ecologica oriented cognitive psychologists have argued that methodologies of tra tional psychology are too restrictive. From our viewpoint psychology h long been handicapped by its almost exclusive reliance on the laborato its restrictive research materials, and its conveniently short (but scienti cally limiting) time periods. We argue for a wide range of "lifelike ma rials," for examining memory in ecologically valid settings, and for rec delays (sometimes as long as decades) that reflect the range and capaci of the human mind. Neuenschwander would surely approve these goals.

Both cognitive psychologists and oral historians advocate blending t new methodologies with the old rather than pressing for the rejection a replacement of the older methodologies, a practice popular among ps chologists, if not historians. They share the belief that the new metho complement the old, that practitioners must be well grounded in both, a that the combined methods yield a more complete and compelling pictu of the world than does either alone. Finally, although both oral history a ecological cognitive psychology reflect old traditions in their discipline both have received renewed scientific attention in recent decades.

The differences between the areas, however, should not be overlooke The cognitive psychologists' interest in formal characteristics or structu of memory contrasts sharply with the oral historians' concern with me ory's contents. This difference between the disciplines is seen clearly their respective attitudes toward errors. Oral historians, on the average, a troubled if their respondents produce error-ridden narratives. Cogniti psychologists, on the other hand, have made errors their stock-in-trad Errors are the tools by which theoretical mechanisms of memory a thought to be revealed. When there are too few errors, psychologis worry about artifacts such as ceiling effects and are likely to reject the da and select more compelling paradigms or, perhaps, better subjects. imagine oral historians resorting to similar strategies when their narrator story displays too many (not too few) errors.

I might have called this paper, "Almost everything I ever wanted to sa to an oral historian." Why did I call it "Phoenix and Chimera"? Memorie we believe, rise like the phoenix from their own ashes: following the sam pattern but always new. *Chimera* I am using in its several senses—to mea both a many-faceted, changing creature as well as a creature of th imagination. The phrase is my announcement that I shall focus o memory's changing face rather than on its stability. To illustrate this poin I have selected three themes that I believe will be of interest to ora historians and not too dull for the psychologists: (1) changes in memor associated with the kind of search that is made (the way in which th narrator addresses memory); (2) changes in memory associated with emo tion; and (3) changes that emerge as our personal memories mature an

e. A memorial fermentation process seems to occur as memories "ripen," en if it is not always a fine wine that results!

I shall be referring to ideas derived from two long-term memory studies volving my own memory. Let me begin by outlining the approaches ed. These studies, sometimes described as "Ebbinghausian" after the ork of that innovative German psychologist of the last century,[3] are still usual among cognitive psychologists. Like Ebbinghaus, I am my princi-l subject, and my studies like his have lasted for many years. My studies, wever, differ importantly from Ebbinghaus's in the kind of material they nploy: Ebbinghaus, who was instrumental in establishing contemporary ychologists' interest in abstract memory, developed and studied onsense syllables" such as DAX and PEF. In contrast, the materials I nploy are highly structured and meaningful. Ebbinghaus continued his ngle-subject research for about five years, but he most often recalled aterials after relatively brief delays. These short delays are a natural nsequence of the stimuli he employed. Recall was so poor after longer riods that he was forced to rely on "savings" methods to discern that e information had been previously known. ("Savings" refers to the de-eased amount of time required to *relearn* forgotten materials compared ith the time originally required.) With real-life events comprising my more eaningful stimuli, it is possible to examine recall after much longer time riods using more standard retention measures.

I inaugurated my long-term memory research in 1972 with a diary-ethod study of my own *autobiographical* memory. Each day for ten ars I entered two to five descriptions of events from my own life into an ver-expanding file of four-by-six cards. Were I entering items contem-raneously, I would surely include an item such as: I present a talk at the lemory and History symposium at Baylor University. Once a month for x of these years, using a variety of tests, I examined my memory for a redetermined sample of these items. A more detailed description of these rocedures appears elsewhere.[4] Among the eleven thousand or more items collected over this ten-year period were numerous events similar to those hich oral historians might elicit from people's memories. It is not too far-tched to imagine that were an oral historian to interview me about an istorical topic—such as "cognitive psychology in the 1970s"—my narra-ve would include some of these items. Because these events are part of rdinary life, they (like memories of interest to oral historians) may be pontaneously rehearsed—that is, I may think or talk about them—or they nay remain relatively neglected.

In 1979 I began a second memory project involving long-term recall for emantic information. The resulting studies explore what I call the maintenance of knowledge."[5] In these studies I began by deliberately earning a carefully selected body of nonpersonal, nonevent information, ne names of plants.

The items learned are tested and rehearsed after increasingly long c
lays. The stimuli for most of these studies have been color pictures
plants while the responses learned are the common, scientific, and fam
names associated with them. Let me highlight the ways in which t
maintenance-of-knowledge studies differ from my autobiographical me
ory study. I shall then explain why I have begun to study these more f
mal stimulus materials. First, real-life event memories are related in a varie
of complex ways; the scientific materials used in the maintenance
knowledge studies are related in relatively simple, formal ways. Each ite
has a comparable set of names. It is as if we have simplified the grammar
produce sentences with subject, verb, and object in a standard fram
Second, there exists an acknowledged correct version of each ite
learned. Third, in my paradigm I memorize this information quite exact
during the learning sessions. Fourth, although information is inevitably lo
over time, the verifiably correct information is reintroduced into memo
through regular rehearsals.

I always hated it when my mathematics professor used the introducto
phrase: "It is obvious that . . . ." I hope, however, that I may show the re
evance of these features of "maintenance of knowledge" to the study
autobiographical memory. Let me begin by considering why it is importa
that the items have comparable structures. First, we assume that comple
schemas or frameworks underlie events in our autobiographical memorie
however, it is difficult to specify these frameworks ad hoc. Ordinarily in m
autobiographical memory studies, forgotten information is simply los
After loss, a lacuna or hole exists in the story. In daily life and i
autobiographical memory studies, when some features of the informatio
are retained, plausible memorial elements may be borrowed from othe
memories to fill existing holes (or empty frames) in the story. Presumabl
these memory elements come from related frameworks. Because it i
difficult to judge similarities among complex autobiographical memor
schemas, it is difficult to predict when or where these migrations will occu
With simpler materials we can perhaps begin to discern how th
substitutions occur. Specifically, I hope that by using systematically relate
materials with standard structures I might observe both how th
informational structure builds up with repetition and how errors relate t
this developing knowledge base. These materials and memories are clearl
not directly comparable to the materials of interest to the oral historians c
autobiographers, but I think that the memory changes observed here she
some light on the way autobiographical memories change.

Second, because there is an established correct version of thes
"simpler" materials, we have much better control over the basic informa
tion in memory. (For even a simple autobiographical memory many addi
tional layers of knowledge may exist.) For these simpler memories it i
much clearer what was learned. Third, both forgetting and rehearsals occu

our naturally occurring memories, but it is difficult to control the number f rehearsals that occur. In the maintenance paradigm, well-defined hearsals can occur at specified intervals. Finally, I can look at the milarities between items and predict what set of errors will intrude when oles" in memories occur.

To summarize, memories of interest to oral historians—those that are metimes rehearsed and sometimes not, those that are sometimes coher- ntly integrated into the remaining memories and sometimes not, those that ometimes may be (and are) verified against existing sources and other mes may not—probably lie somewhere between the psychologists' emantic knowledge (my maintenance-of-knowledge studies) and episodic emories (my autobiographical studies). I hope by alluding to both lines of esearch to illumine some dark corners of oral history. I begin with ideas elated to my autobiographical memory research. Some of these specific leas have been described at greater length in my paper "Ways of earching and the Contents of Memory."[6]

THE STABILITY OF OUR INTERNAL HISTORIES

SOME METHODS FOR ACCESSING THE CONTENTS OF THE MIND

When something occurs, does the event create a single (unique) repre- entation in our memory? Contemporary cognitive psychologists argue gainst such an idea. They believe that propositions (or fundamental mem- ry units) are stored in memory together with some organizing algorithms. rom these elements a new creation, an abstraction, a new representation f the original memory, is reconstructively derived on each recall occasion. hus, we can see that not only is memory a chimera, a creature of many spects, but like the phoenix it arises anew from its propositional ashes at ach recall.

How stable are our internal histories? How alike are our chimeric hoenixes? Or, less poetically, what variables control the reconstructions ve obtain? Among other variables, the *kind of interrogation* may influ- nce how general or specific the recall is, may control the extent to which letails are included or omitted, and indeed (as we shall see) may influence he content. Perhaps Daniel McCall[7] did not go far enough when he sug- gested that "There will be as many histories as historians"; it is perhaps nore accurate to suggest a unique history for every condition of recall.

To summarize: Memory's contents are much more complex than any particular individual articulation of them; each verbal statement represent- ing the contents or structure of memory requires a reconstructive process, and this process and its products are likely to differ from one occasion to the next. In the following pages, moving from unconstrained to con-

strained methods, I consider some effects of the way in which informati
is accessed.

Thoughts that come unbidden. Throughout my life I have not
delicate memory fragments that recur year after year—coming unbidde
sometimes when my "mind is silent" (this language is Esther Salaman's
but also occasionally as by-products of searches for other informatio
Some of these fragments are epigrammatic. They sometimes requi
interpretation, as might a proverb, and other times remain uninterpretab
Sometimes the crux of my relationship with a person spanning years
decades may be encapsulated in a series of such fragments. The
epigrammatic "unbidden" memories are often more accessible when
"float about" in memories for individuals or themes than when
deliberately "search." The items produced by this kind of reverie a
strikingly different from those produced by deliberate searches. They a
more fragmentary and less episodic. Their minimal overlap with standa
listings underlines how sensitive our accessed memory contents are to th
methods we employ.

Would these "tidbits" ever occur in a description given to an oral his
torian? Perhaps not. They are more like the memories elicited by a psy
chiatrist. Perhaps they are too personal, too homey, too epigrammatic, an
too rambling to be shared except under special circumstances. Becaus
they are unorganized, they are poorly tied to or interconnected with othe
memories. If an omniscient interviewer asked why these details were nc
included in my accounts, I might truthfully respond, "They never occurre
to me." Salaman also suggests that they are associated with a "crystallin
emotion,"[9] and indeed some of mine are quite embarrassing. Even if th
natural organization of the memory did not render this informatio
unavailable to an orderly memory search, one's internal editor migh
intervene to prevent the information from being reported to a questioner
These memories serve a function in our personal histories, but it is not clea
how relevant these apparently disconnected bits are to a more genera
history.

Many oral historians, who know they may obtain new information i
the narrator rambles on for a bit, have struggled with achieving a balanc
between the focus of the interview and the potential risk of losing fres
information if the meandering narrative is prematurely terminated. The ris
of information being lost is perhaps greatest when the recall is of well
practiced information driven by a well-defined scheme. But musing ove
old memories is most often left to older individuals[10] or younger ones ir
rare moments of repose. Most certainly musing or reverie are not ordinaril
used by psychologist or historian to acquire information from memory
Aside from violating certain social expectations, these methods are quite
slow and inefficient and have uncertain payoff.

Temporally cued free recall. To efficiently access specific classes of memories somewhat more structure is required. The most minimal prompt to memory is probably a temporal one. The broader the temporal range specified, the fewer constraints are placed on memory. In reminiscing among friends, we may dredge up "when I was a child . . ." memories. Mimicking this procedure experimentally, I have asked myself, for example: "Tell me everything you remember from 1976 or 1980," and so on.

Given an appropriate date, precisely how does one find memories? One hops, skips, and jumps through memorial landmarks searching for one that coincides with some discernable date. I often do this by moving through what I have called "extendures," easily referenced, longer, unified periods of my life.[11] Where was I working? Where was I living? Who were my significant others? I then move from these broad units to narrower ones. I can usually, with time and effort, develop a plausible set of activities to coincide with time periods (my choice of the word *plausible* rather than *accurate* is deliberate).

Note that this task is different from and somewhat easier than the converse task, recalling dates associated with events. On this point, Lang and Mercier comment, "Interviewers and narrators alike sometimes expect accurate recall of dates, but most people do not remember their lives in terms of calendar years or specific months. More often, people look at their lives with little or no sense of chronology and associate time—even the passage of time—primarily with memorable events."[12]

While they are quite correct that oral history is not an appropriate method to establish chronology in history, some individuals do deal quite competently with dates. Moreover, virtually all individuals can improve their ability to date by searching for landmarks against which to place target memories.

A final comment on temporal cues: I have suggested that dates do not directly color or cue specific memory contents. Robinson, using recent months as cues, has shown that some months (for example, those associated with the beginning and end of school) are more effective as cues than others.[13] Moreover, Robinson argues that the schema associated with each month vary and that quite different internal cues are elicited by specifying particular months. Thus, for months and probably for days of the week as well, time cues do provide significant information about activities that might have occurred.

A more exact specification—for example, cuing by topic—may dramatically change the memorial contents available from any period.

Categorical recall. How easily can we access our memories with temporal or categorical cues? I found a curious partial answer to this question when I analyzed a series of recall protocols[14] in which I provided a time cue and sought to list items from memory that were from one month to twelve years old. In the study that involved periods of less than one year, I *always* sought to recall items by using simple chronological searches. When longer delays were involved (for example, searches for material as old as twelve years), chronological searches were preferred only when information was recalled from recent periods. Specifically, for delays as long as thirty months I was able to quickly and accurately access a wide variety of information with no more than the month and the year as a cue. For periods longer than thirty months, I found no evidence of chronological searches. For longer delays I resorted to categorical searches (that is, I created or selected categories of events and then conducted my search for memories within them). The abrupt transition from chronological to categorical searches was puzzling. In an effort to understand whether this abrupt shift was optional, I attempted to chronologically access information from the longer periods. After repeated efforts it became clear that, at least for the conditions of the study, information from the longer periods was not available through a chronological search. Categorical cues were *required* to access information older than thirty months. You may understand this difference if you consider how you would describe today's activities: It is very easy to begin with, I got up, I ate breakfast; that is, it is easy to simply chain the events together. For all of us, after a day, a week, a month, or thirty months, we lose the chronology and are forced to rely on categorical searches.

Considerably greater constraints are imposed by the requirement to search memory within categories—broad or narrow. Thus, categorical recall is simpler than less constrained searches because it permits us to focus our internal gaze, and to limit our search. Although none of my own methods formally impose categorical limitations, my self-generated categories greatly simplify searches.

Considering the oral historian again, complex cues—combining temporal with categorical cues—may well be provided. What can one do with a topic and a time? "Tell me about desegregation activities in 1958," for example, might provide the skeleton for an appropriate cue. It seems likely, moreover, that an implicit starting point with respect to locale (probably wherever you were at that time) may be imposed if a more explicit location is not; for example, "Tell me about desegregation activities in 1958 *in New Orleans*."

Cued recall. The cues provided by the psychologist or historian to prompt target memories are likely to become increasingly more specific as an interview proceeds. It is likely that the completeness and exactness of recall is ultimately dependent on the specificity and aptness of the cues provided. Using a succession of cues may yield more information and would probably mimic natural usage more closely. Successive cuing provides an analogue to a natural procedure that we all recognize. Skilled conversationalists, in attempting to renew a friend's old memories, may try successively more specific cues: "Do you remember when we . . . ?" "No." "Remember, we were rowing on the lead raft . . . " et cetera. Most natural searches yield some consensus between conversationalists, and these multiple cues are more effective than the original discrete ones in producing a match. The effectiveness of any particular class of cues probably depends on the target memory and the particular memorist.

Wagenaar, in a research design that replicates and extends my own autobiographical memory study, has recently examined the effectiveness of specific elements of a memory as cues.[15] In particular he was concerned with people, action, place, or time as cues in eliciting memories. These he calls *who, what, where,* and *when*. Across his various events, Wagenaar sequentially presented his four cues in all possible twenty-four orders. Given any single cue or multiple cues, he therefore could determine the probability that the remaining target information was produced. He found that the differences produced by order of presentation were almost as large as those produced by retention period. A very powerful effect indeed! The most successful orders, those in which *what* was given first, followed by *when*, elicited approximately 60 percent correct responses. In the least successful orders—those in which *when* came first followed by *who* or *where*—fewer than 30 percent of the responses were correct.

Wagenaar also examined the efficacy of single cues. He found that *what* alone was very powerful and that *when* alone was almost useless. He ordered the cues in value: what, where, who, and when. Wagenaar argues quite reasonably that the uniqueness of the specific cues is the crucial factor. While some of the discrepancies between his results and my own are due to important methodological differences, those regarding the value of temporal cues may be due to individual differences.

Recognition. Recognition is almost always more accurate than recall when tests are done in the laboratory. It is not clear how fully this result extends to autobiography and history. Recognizing a picture or a word seen before is almost certainly very different from "recognizing" an event. One cannot show or "say" events or episodes. Any representation of events or episodes must be more abstract and symbolic than the event itself. In my autobiographical memory study I represented events with brief verbal descriptions that I had written. In a variation on this theme, several researchers have asked other individuals to record events for their subjects. People perform considerably less well when asked to recognize items created by someone else. Dealing appropriately with items generated by someone else is always problematic. Salaman comments interestingly on descriptions provided by others:

> It has happened many times that as soon as I have told a memory to persons who have memories of the same period I am immediately asked if I remember other moments—things which they remember about me. I am often interested, amused and sometimes flattered, but when pressed to recognise the events I feel almost hostile. Other people's memories of us no more belong to us than their dreams of us.[16]

In the preceding material I have tried (using the metaphor of the chimeric phoenix) to suggest that our reconstructions from memory are potentially enormously diverse. And while we may create standard representations to instantiate past events, ordinarily our recall of past events is capable of endless variation depending on our motivations and procedures for reactivating the memories.

AFFECT

Other things being equal, is one more likely to remember events that are happy (or pleasant), or events that are sad (or unpleasant)? A variety of studies employing a range of materials and subjects have demonstrated that positive events or memories are better recalled than negative. The finding is so general that Matlin and Stang were able to title a book on the subject *The Pollyanna Principle*.[17] Most research by cognitive psychologists has supported this result and it appears almost impervious to challenge. But how inconvenient such a conclusion is to the oral historian! Let us consider the nature of these results and their relevance for oral historians.

These studies consistently show that affect has a profound effect on recall[18] but a lesser one (or perhaps none) on recognition. Specifically, one should be less likely to *recall* negative (or disturbing information) than positive information. Confirming these results, examination of my recall protocols indicates that negative events from my own life are largely omitted. Many negative events from the past were nevertheless instantly recognized, with good corroborative detail, in "recognition" sessions even when they fail to appear in general recall protocols. That is, I cannot (or do not) always access the negative information, but such information is available with a little prompting.

One explanation for the absence of negative items appearing in recall protocols is that negative items (for reasons discussed at length by Matlin and Stang) are less well imbedded in the underlying scheme of one's life. One may argue, for example, that an accident, hurt feelings, embarrassment may not be rehearsed as often or may not have consequences that assure they are unforgettable.

We must, however, reconcile with these findings the quite different results from well-known public events. Most general news events are not well remembered. But what about the public events that interface with our private lives? For example, it is likely that the best-remembered public events of the last fifty years are the bombing of Pearl Harbor and the assassination of John F. Kennedy.[19] There are a number of explanations for the superior recallability of these events. First, it can be argued that these events are exceptionally emotional. A comparable personal event might be a death or disaster in one's own life. While such personal events are probably not forgotten, they rarely come within the psychologist's purview. Second, these events provided, and for many still provide "benchmarks"[20] in the lives of individuals who experienced them. And indeed, although public or news events are typically not well integrated into the schemata of our personal lives, for most individuals these classic items are closely tied to personal recollections. Almost all people, in response to inquiries about these crucial events, begin by personally locating themselves physically and psychologically with respect to the event. Perhaps this integration occurs because of the very human tendency to move oneself to the center of important action (this is poignantly illustrated by Neisser in his description of John Dean's Watergate testimony).[21] Perhaps these dramatically negative items are more heroic and hence are less susceptible to deletion than are the negative events in our own lives. Perhaps they are remembered because each changed our lives and the fate of the nation so completely. Perhaps dramatic negative events are more easily recalled because they receive greater media coverage (and concomitant rehearsal), or because one is not remembering a single event but a whole complex of events. Large configurations in memory are considerably more difficult to overlook than small events might be.

Need the oral historian be concerned that negatively toned events may be less accessible to the narrator than other events? Although not all the evidence is in, it seems likely that the principles governing recall of negative public events may be very different from those psychologists have discovered govern recall of negative personal events and that one must consider the balance struck in the event between personal and public memory elements.

In a related inquiry, the oral historian may sometimes want to know how the narrator felt about some past event at the time of its occurrence. Affect is sufficiently complex that, with a single event, relatively positive affect may be accessed with one interrogation and relatively negative affect with another. Moreover, it is not unusual for reported affect to change *over time*,[22] with the *current affect* of the narrator,[23] and possibly with the *specific cues* provided by the researcher.

I have argued that affect for past events is itself chimerical.[24] When an event occurs, individuals respond with a set of emotions (let us call these the "original emotions"). Sometimes these emotions are simple, sometimes complex (for example, anger and fear may be combined). Over time however, the internal historian conducts her business of summarizing, interpreting, and editing, and the events take on new or different meaning. Changes occur in our lives and as a result some event or person important to our lives a decade ago may be of diminished importance now. Most events become more neutral with the passage of time. Quite surprisingly, even strong positive or negative emotions are likely to become more neutral. The analogy that suggests itself to those of us who have just moved a household is that of unpacking boxes of goods we haven't seen for months or years. It is not always clear why items were precious enough to be carefully wrapped and repeatedly moved. Many items (like our memories, perhaps) have lost their importance. It is a very rare event (often one of great emotional importance) that retains high affective levels over time. Perhaps the effect observed by statisticians—that extremely high test scores are usually not repeated—may be related to this effect. This phenomenon, the regression to the mean, is thought to occur because a very unusual combination of events is necessary to produce an outstanding score in the first place and this fortuitous combination is not likely to be reproduced on later occasions. (For example, you have studied carefully, you are well rested, et cetera.) Fortuitous changes in the remembered elements may change the extremity of emotion just as analogous changes affect test scores.

Although it happens less often, occasionally our memories become more affectively charged. An event that looks trivial when it occurs may be imbued with retroactive importance; it may take on significance that makes it extremely emotional. That is, as we continue to rewrite our own histories, some old events are rewritten in ways that we would not have guessed when they occurred.

Let me summarize the significance of these affective issues to the oral historian: (1) Although most positive events are better recalled than negative, the data are not all in. Additional research may be needed to determine whether public events may have a special status. Perhaps negative emotionality does *not* impair recall for public as it does private events; (2) Individuals' assessment of emotionality for long-past events is not always reliable. As Lang and Mercier suggest: "There is often a shift in mood and emphasis in the narrator's answers when questions stimulate a tug-of-war between long-term memory and subsequent feelings about an event."[25] (3) And a final issue: high expressed emotionality does not assure high recall accuracy. It is well documented that many of the forces associated with emotional memories act to degrade them.

CHANGES THAT OCCUR IN MEMORY OVER TIME

I have considered changes in reported memory resulting from different interrogations of memory, and from the impact of emotions. I shall address one final issue: changes–either in the form of memory losses or other transformations—that take place in memory over time.

Ebbinghaus used nonsense syllables to demonstrate rapid loss from memory at first and slower loss later. Most syllables could not be remembered after hours or days. It is not clear how relevant this classic result is for the more meaningful materials and much longer delays of the oral historian. A result that is likely to have greater relevance emerged from my autobiographical memory research. I found that autobiographical events were lost at the almost linear rate of 6 percent a year after an initial year or so during which very little loss occurred. Researchers in two replications of this study suggest that information is lost even more rapidly (these differences are undoubtedly due both to individual and methodological differences). Indeed, the notion of continued loss at that rate does not bear too close scrutiny! However, it is evident to even casual introspection that some kinds of information are readily lost while others are more resilient.

It is difficult to assess how crucial this kind of loss might be for the oral historian's narrator. What kind of information is lost and what recalled? Let me shift the scene slightly and consider the kind of changes we believe may occur in memory. Cognitive psychologists have found it convenient to distinguish two kinds of information in memory: episodic and semantic knowledge. Although this distinction is flawed[26] we shall maintain it in this brief discussion. Episodic knowledge refers to memories that are "one of a kind," for example, a particular walk in the woods; while semantic knowledge refers to general memories, for example the general knowledge derived from those many walks in Burnham Beeches.

It seems to me that oral historians are, at different times, likely to be interested in either kind of memory. Moreover, different kinds of research problems require reliance upon different aspects of memory. The oral historian might, for example, be interested in the general working conditions in an industry forty years ago (semantic). He or she might equally well try to document a particular sequence of events at that time (episodic). It is here that I believe my work on maintenance of knowledge may ultimately provide some insights. Memory is chimerical—but its rule of transition is not mystical or magical.

Let me remind you of my study: for many years I have learned the names of plants (an orderly set of material, indeed much more orderly than the materials of the historian). Let me give you a specific item:

True forget-me-not
Myosotis scorpioides
Forget-me-not family (*Boraginaceae*)

These are, respectively, the common name, genus, and species, and in the final line, the English and Latin versions of the family name. These materials are memorized until they are probably more familiar to me than many events in my own life. Following this encoding, a period of time passes before recall is required, just as it does for natural memories. How does the memory perform after these delays when I see the unique cue—the picture of the plant?

What kind of errors occur? In the beginning, the highly familiar common names are easily recalled and the more difficult Latin names are rapidly forgotten and are rarely given correctly. Almost all the errors occur on these latter items. With repeated rehearsals, however, the family names become easier and easier to recall. Moreover, this is true both for the relatively easy English "forget-me-not," and for the Latin *Boraginaceae*. At this point, as the family names are well fixed in memory, I begin to find errors predictable from what Rosch calls "family resemblances."[27] If the flower "looks like a sunflower," you call it a sunflower even if you have learned that it belongs to another family. At this point in the fermentation process, the individual's general (or semantic) knowledge powerfully controls recall. Presumably such forces caused a friend to substitute my name for that of her real companion when many years later she described her activities at the time of J. F. Kennedy's death.

My data suggest that virtually all errors in my "expert memory" involve substitution of highly probable and highly accessible family names into frames left vacant by failures to recall less frequent family names. Moreover, rare families and untypical members of more common families are usually the ones for which the substitutions occur. Children make the same kinds of mistakes as they learn language, at first using irregular words correctly (for example, "I made it"), and then beginning to make mistakes ("I maked it") as they learn the rules of language, and ultimately coming to use the words in the standard adult way. To be explicit about my beliefs on natural memory, I believe that in ordinary recall common routines are substituted for less common ones, well-known individuals are substituted for less well-known ones, and that times migrate to make coherent stories. Information too complex or too unusual to be coded efficiently is deleted.

In this paper I have highlighted some areas in which the research of psychologists may articulate with the concerns of the oral historian. I have argued for the fluidity of memory, and while my suggestion of one memory for every recall condition is probably an exaggeration, a wide range of instantiations are deemed "satisfactory recall" both by the narrator and the oral historian.

Emotional fragments which comprise many of the pieces of the historical jigsaw provide many special problems in recall. Recall of how you "felt" about something in the past undergoes distortions as do other memories. Understanding the intersections of positive and negative with public and private events over very long periods of time provides a most interesting challenge to the combined talents of psychologists and oral historians.

Finally, I have hinted at ways in which semantic knowledge may govern production of memory errors. Highly probable terms appear to move from locations in one set of items into comparable locations (where less familiar material has been deleted) in other items. Through a combination of these mechanisms with many others that psychologists have studied and described, memories simplify themselves.

Memory's face gradually changes and becomes—perhaps—history. To use Neuenschwander's language as he describes the research of Bartlett, "The end product was not so much a distortion of the original as a simpler, more functional rendition."[28] Or as Marc Bloch admonished, "Have patience. History is not yet what it ought to be."[29]

Notes

1. John Neuenschwander, "Remembrance of Things Past: Oral Historians and Long-Term Memory," *Oral History Review* 6 (1978): 45-53.

2. Ibid., 49.

3. Hermann Ebbinghaus, *Memory*, trans. Henry A. Ruger and Clara E. Bussenius (New York: Dover, 1964).

4. Marigold Linton, "Memory for Real-World Events," in *Explorations in Cognition*, ed. Donald A. Norman and David E. Rumelhart (San Francisco: W. . Freeman, 1975), 376-404; Marigold Linton, "Real-World Memory after Six Years: An In Vivo Study of Very Long-Term Memory," in *Practical Aspects of Memory*, ed. M. M. Gruneberg, P. E. Morris, and R. N. Sykes (London: Academic Press, 1979), 69-76; Marigold Linton, "Transformations of Memory in Everyday Life," in *Memory Observed: Remembering in Natural Contexts*, ed. Ulric Neisser (San Francisco: W. H. Freeman, 1982), 77-91.

5. Marigold Linton, "The Maintenance of Knowledge: Some Long-Term Specific and Generic Changes," in *Practical Aspects of Memory: Current Research and Issues, Vol. I. Memory in Everyday Life*, ed. M. M. Gruneberg, P. E. Morris, and R. N. Sykes (New York: Wiley, 1988).

6. Marigold Linton, "Ways of Searching and the Contents of Memory" in *Autobiographical Memory*, ed. David C. Rubin (New York: Cambridge University Press, 1986), 50-67.

7. Alphine W. Jefferson, "Echoes from the South: The History and Methodology of the Duke University Oral History Program," *Oral History Review* 12 (1984): 52.

8. Esther Salaman, *A Collection of Moments: A Study of Involuntary Memorie* (London: Longman Group, 1970).
9. Ibid.
10. Ibid.
11. Linton, "Ways of Searching and the Contents of Memory."
12. William L. Lang and Laurie K. Mercier, "Getting It Down Right: Ora History's Reliability in Local History Research," *Oral History Review* 12 (1984): 81 99.
13. J. A. Robinson, "The Temporal Organization of Autobiographical Memory," in *Autobiographical Memory*, ed. Rubin, 159-80.
14. Linton, "Ways of Searching and the Contents of Memory."
15. Willem A. Wagenaar, "My Memory: A Study of Autobiographical Memory Over Six Years," *Cognitive Psychology* 18 (1986): 225-52.
16. Salaman, *A Collection of Moments*, 112.
17. Margaret W. Matlin and David J. Stang, *The Pollyanna Principle: Selectivity in Language, Memory and Thought* (Cambridge, Mass.: Schenkman, 1978).
18. G. H. Bower, "Mood and Memory," *American Psychologist* 36 (1981): 129-48.
19. R. Brown and J. Kulik, "Flashbulb Memories," *Cognition* 5 (1977): 73-79.
20. Ulric Neisser, "Snapshots or Benchmarks?," in *Memory Observed,* ed. Neisser, 43-48.
21. Ulric Neisser, "John Dean's Memory: A Case Study," *Cognition* 9 (1981): 1-22.
22. Linton, "Transformations of Memory in Everyday Life."
23. Bower, "Mood and Memory."
24. Linton, "Transformations of Memory in Everyday Life" and "Ways of Searching and the Contents of Memory."
25. Lang and Mercier, "Getting It Down Right," 95.
26. For example, see A. Richardson-Klavehn and R. A. Bjork, "Measures of Memory," *Annual Review of Psychology* 39 (1988): 475-543.
27. E. Rosch and C. B. Mervis, "Family Resemblances: Studies in the Internal Structure of Categories," *Cognitive Psychology* 7 (1975): 79-99.
28. Neuenschwander, "Remembrances of Things Past," 48.
29. Marc Bloch, *The Historian's Craft* (New York: Vintage Books, 1953), 67.

COMMENT

Kim Lacy Rogers *is a professor of history at Dickinson College who has focused much of her work in oral history on the Civil Rights movement. Here she explores the potential for using the principles of memory theory described by Lin-*

n to understand the ways in which individuals find meaning in their life experi-ıces.

In "Memory as Chimera: The Changing Face of Memory," as in other ublished works, Marigold Linton discusses the different forms that mem-ry takes in structure and organization, the different kinds of searches that ıdividuals employ to retrieve specific memories, and the reliability of ifferent kinds of memories.

I would like to discuss the relevance of Linton's categories of memory) the oral historian's work. As oral historians, we gather information from arrators about both objective events—moments in public, "official" istory—and subjective events and perceptions—the personal interpreta-ions of historical experience. Linton's work in autobiographical memory as particular relevance for those of us who study individual lives and heir autobiographical "reconstruction"—the retrospectively arranged atterns of coherence that all of us make into our life histories. These ret-ospective arrangements can and often do differ with the passage of time, nd with the addition of new and sometimes radically discontinuous expe-ience. We know that individuals who have survived natural disasters, vars, or harrowing personal experiences often find their lives redirected or 'changed utterly" by the extremities of emotional experience associated vith dislocation and trauma. Linton's work suggests a structure or schema vith which we might attempt to understand the connections between ontinuity and discontinuity in personal and collective life, and the etrospective rearrangement of "benchmark" or "symbolic" experiences s lives change.[1]

First, Linton distinguishes episodic memory from semantic (or general) nowledge memory. In a 1982 article, she writes, "increased experience vith any particular event class increases semantic . . . knowledge about the vent and its context. Increased experience with similar events, however, nakes specific episodic knowledge increasingly confusable, and ultimately pisodes cannot be distinguished."[2] This can explain the inability of narrators to "get" dates and events right, while they retain broad general knowledge of historical transformation or of a specific culture. Thus, the episodic memories, though building blocks of the larger semantic structures, are often lost, or confused by repetition, while a richly textured "knowledge" memory remains.

Oral historians who work with manuscript collections and documents as well as with oral testimony are in a more advantaged position when in-terviewing narrators than are those interviewers who do not possess this documentary backup. With an adequate evidentiary base, it is often possi-ble to obtain the episodic structures of the semantic knowledge and to ask

a narrator specific "cued" questions directed toward the specifics of tim
and incident that might otherwise remain "lost" within memory. Linto
suggests that "multiple cues" are "more effective than discrete ones" i
producing a recall from a narrator. Thus, an interviewer with good his
torical knowledge, and perhaps employing a two-question format, woul
almost certainly be more successful than a questioner who did not ap
proach a narrator with careful research and a biographically grounde
format.[3]

Linton also suggests that memories change with the contemporar
emotion experienced by the individual: "Positive events or memories ar
better recalled than negative." This finding is "so pervasive" that Matli
and Stang labeled it a "Pollyanna Principle." Linton points out that whil
the "forgetting" of the negative seems to be a common human response t
pain, "it is a very rare event (often one of great emotional importance) tha
retains high effective levels over time."

This is an interesting finding, given the numbers of oral historians wh
have interviewed and studied individuals who have experienced extrem
discontinuities in their lives, and often strongly negative experiences tha
came to assume a symbolic importance in their autobiographical narratives
I am thinking here of the oral narratives of two civil rights lawyers
interviewed in 1978 and 1979. A black lawyer had dated his disillusion
ment with the integrationist aims of black intellectuals to a realization tha
all of the civil rights organizations were white-controlled. White domina
tion of a black liberation movement made him question the goals and aim
of moderate black elites and to embrace Muslim nationalism as an ideolog
ical solution to black oppression.[4] Similarly, a white lawyer had dated th
"hardening" of his own attitudes toward segregationists to an evening i
which he had given a speech to his civic group, explaining the unconstitu
tionality of Louisiana's statutes of interposition. His friends and neighbor
grew angry and walked out. Both men used these negative memories t
mark a symbolic change and transformation of their lives, of forcing new
decisions and allegiances. Their identities as activists were, in part, created
by those negative events that each remembered in later years.[5]

The retention of negative events in these two oral narratives raises
questions about the relation of semantic memory to episodic and the role
of the negative event in provoking or determining personal growth and
development. When *do* negative events become benchmarks of personal
growth? Among civil rights activists, black and white leaders related numerous negative memories which were frequently paired with positive,
self-affirming solutions to the problematic event. Is this dialectic of personal growth—one rooted in struggle—only the province of the political
activist? Or is it a more common structure among individuals? And if, as
Jerome Bruner has suggested, we project ourselves into the future through
the self-concepts embedded in our life histories and autobiographical

ıemories, what kind of projection would be produced by a dialectic of egative event: positive resolution, pain and denial: personal growth?[6]

Linton has suggested that "strong positive or negative emotions are kely to become more neutral" with the passage of time and that "as we ontinue to rewrite our own histories, old events come to be rewritten in ays that we would not have guessed at the time of their occurrence.")ral historians who are sensitive to changes in individual psychology over ıe life span should find these statements intriguing. We know that we rogressively reconstruct our lives as we add new experiences, whether ıey are transformative or not. However, are we as sensitive as we should e to the impact of a narrator's age on his or her reconstruction of experince, history, and meaning? Esther Salaman has indicated that older vomen and men have a different sense of biographical recall than do ounger autobiographers; particularly, older people often have more vivid unbidden" memories of childhood and early years.[7]

If, as life-course scholars suggest, the years after age sixty are marked y reconciliation and acceptance, would not an older person demonstrate more subdued emotional cast to a personal narrative than would a ıarrator interviewed at mid-life? How are we to assess the relative value, or veight, of conflict or discontinuity versus stability in shaping both a life ınd a historical interpretation of that life? If "individuals are more likely to emember information that is congruent or consistent with their own riginal mood," might, then, the individual's age—his or her stage in the ife-course—determine in major ways the color, tone, feeling, and events of ecollection? Might not individuals at mid-life be more restless, more onflict-oriented than older narrators, who might—in the process of ntrospection and reflection—offer a more reconciled view of their own ives and history? My interviews of 1978-1980 bore this out. Even when older activists had experienced disruptive episodes of conflict, each evealed a tendency to pair these episodes to a successful reconciliation vith historical change, which signified—in personal and political terms—he adjustment of the larger political system to their own ideals and goals.[8]

Finally, Linton's work raises questions about the relationship between semantic and episodic memory within the geography of autobiography. Knowing that we retrospectively recreate and reorder our biographies over time, and knowing that discontinuous experiences can change dramatically our interpretation of the shape and meaning of our lives, should we not expect the discontinuities of experience to be reflected in the retention of episodic memories within the general semantic memories that give us identity? In other words, could we not expect that discontinuous experiences might provoke a different geography of episodic memory for the autobiography—that within the same body of semantic memory, different life experiences would increase the contemporary salience of different episodic events, coloring them

differently, giving them different meaning over the course of life? And th
perhaps, over the life-course involved, the most interesting question mig
consider the relationships between the symbolic structures of episod
memory as they change over time: Do we remember different events
symbolic and important as our lives change? Is it possible to chart th
geography of event and meaning in autobiographical narratives
individuals age, experience discontinuity, or stabilize their person
histories in a long process of reflection and reconciliation?

Notes

1. See Marigold Linton, "Transformations of Memory in Everyday Life," ar Ulric Neisser, "Snapshots or Benchmarks?," in *Memory Observed: Remembering Natural Contexts,* ed. Ulric Neisser (San Francisco: W. H. Freeman, 1982), 77-91, 4 48. See also Kim Lacy Rogers, "Memory, Struggle and Power: On Interviewin Political Activists," *Oral History Review* 15 (Spring 1987): 165-84.
2. Linton, "Transformations of Memory in Everyday Life."
3. Kim Lacy Rogers, "Biographical Reconstruction and the Interpretation of Civ Rights Activism," paper presented to the annual meeting of the Oral Histor Association, St. Paul, Minnesota, 16 October 1987. See also Charles T. Morrisse "The Two-Sentence Format as Interviewing Technique in Oral History Fieldwork, *Oral History Review* 15 (Spring 1987): 43-54.
4. Kim Lacy Rogers, "'What We Say Together Is Important': Subculture Socialization, and the Life-Course of Civil Rights Leaders" (unpublished mss.).
5. Kim Lacy Rogers, "Lawyers' Stories: White Attorneys and the Black Civi Rights Movement," paper presented to the Sixth International Oral Histor Conference, Oxford, Great Britain, 11-13 September 1987.
6. Rogers, "Biographical Reconstruction"; Jerome Bruner, "Life as Narrative, *Social Research* 54 (Spring 1987): 11-32.
7. Esther Salaman, "A Collection of Moments," in *Memory Observed,* ed Neisser, 49-63.
8. Kim Lacy Rogers, "Organizational Experience and Personal Narrative: Storie of New Orleans' Civil Rights Leadership," *Oral History Review* 13 (1985): 23-54.

WHAT ONE CANNOT REMEMBER MISTAKENLY

Karen E. Fields

Director of the Frederick Douglass Institute for African and African-American Studies at the University of Rochester, Karen E. Fields is a sociologist who has specialized in the sociology of religion and the sociology of development, particularly in East and Central Africa. A former volunteer teacher in Tanzania and author of Revival and Rebellion in Colonial Central Africa *(1985), Fields developed an interest in African-American family memory through her work with her grandmother Mamie Garvin Fields on* Lemon Swamp and Other Places: A Carolina Memoir *(1983). In* Lemon Swamp, *Fields blends the scholarly with the personal, addressing the tensions between family and professional loyalties to produce a work meaningful in both spheres. In this paper she discusses that process, placing individual memory into its cultural context "to glean from personal testimony the movement of history."*

I chose this title deliberately to provoke. Nothing is more fully agreed than the certainty that memory fails. Memory fails, leaving blanks, and memory collaborates with forces separate from actual past events, forces such as an individual's wishes, a group's suggestions, a moment's connotations, an environment's clues, an emotion's demands, a self's evolution, a mind's manufacture of order, and yes, even a researcher's objectives. In these collaborations, and in others I have not thought of, memory acquires well-noted imperfections. We seek to understand these imperfections systematically if we are scholars of memory in itself, and we seek to correct for them if we are scholars who use memory as a source. As researchers, we bind ourselves to skepticism about memory and to a definite methodological mistrust of rememberers who are our informants. We are fully attentive to the fact that memory fails.

But memory also succeeds. It succeeds enormously and profoundly; for it is fundamental to human life, not to say synonymous with it. A large capacity for memory is an integral component of the complex brain that sets homo sapiens apart. And, without it, the social life that is characteristic of our species would be inconceivable. Thus Nietzsche spoke of memory in terms of our human ability to make, deliver, and collect upon enduring agreements, an ability from which much if not all else is constructed.[1] S although nothing is more certain than that memory fails, equally, nothing more certain than that memory succeeds. Systematic thought about how succeeds, and at what, is thus as much in order as the reverse. Otherwis we who turn to it as a resource fall into paradox.

My work with my grandmother, Mamie Garvin Fields, in her memo *Lemon Swamp and Other Places*, offers me a starting point for reflectic about what memory succeeds in doing and about the ways in which does its work, for it is important to refine continually our methods c observing and thinking about memory as a matter of scholarly or scientifi enterprise. However, I will also reflect a bit upon this sort of enterpris itself, for it is equally important to refine continually our awareness c certain oddities and particularities that shape this enterprise and th therefore shape our inner attitude as we go about our work. As researcher we systematically doubt what we systematically count upon as ordinar human beings in the routine of daily life.

One of the particularities of the enterprise is the paradox we flirt wit when we turn, with methodological mistrust, to memory as a source. Thi danger was present from the beginning of my work on *Lemon Swamp*. turned to my grandmother as a source about the past, aspects of which had few or no other ways of knowing. The book deals with public an private events (from submarine infiltration during World War II to he marriage just before World War I), attributes and assumptions current in he milieu (from race consciousness to notions of proper dress), aspiration (from racial "uplift" to middle-class consumption), judgments bot collective and personal (Who is an Uncle Tom? To whom is a moral perso accountable?), habits about the body (from details of housekeeping t color consciousness), natural and man-made objects in Charleston an elsewhere (from Calhoun's statue on the Citadel green to Lemon Swam itself), and much else.

At the time of working on this rich material, I liberated myself from the constraints of scholarship or science by refusing to call it sociology, history, or even *oral* history. (The constraints tightened no less if I added to "history" the modifier "oral.") Grandmother's term for what we were about was "stories" (and I will say something about stories later on); in the end, we settled for the term *memoir—Lemon Swamp and Other Places: A Carolina Memoir*. I made this liberation clear in the introduction to the book by saying "It is a subjective, personal account of life and work in South Carolina from 1888 to now."[2] Nonetheless, the two of us then, no less than the reading audience we imagined, thought of it as a source about the past. And since I was trained as a sociologist and had done historical research, this liberation remained incomplete. It was not possible for me to run methodological red lights unself-consciously—although I most certainly ran them. The running of them occasioned reflection about what some of the green lights permit.

Consider, for example, the predicament that arises when we treat informants with the methodological mistrust that is required. A special existential condition arises between two human beings communicating face to face. Contrary to the "face value" methodology of everyday human encounters, ours requires skepticism, suspicion, a certain condescension, and above all a constantly open second channel in which to place those bits of testimony that are destined to float out of the interaction, back toward some source of corroboration. This is alien to normal human communication. (The closest everyday-life kin to it involves police and special agents.) Equally alien to everyday life is the patronizing of an interlocutor with silent knowingness when other information establishes that he or she is wrong or even lying. Suppressing the social commonplaces of contradiction, correction, or dismissal belongs to that special existential condition I am talking about, the one our methodological green lights permit. Now, if the condition of gaining knowledge is first to create a surrogate of human interaction, thereafter deliberately to diminish it, this proceeding demands its own scrutiny—quite apart from the scrutiny the testimony itself gets. This scrutiny amounts to examining our tools in order to see clearly what they are accomplishing above and beyond our intended purpose. When a surgeon sterilizes the knife with which he cuts through flesh in order to repair the heart, he nevertheless still has to attend to the knife's secondary achievements.

I ran the red light that blocks arguing with an informant. Liberated from the constraints of scholarship, I said to Gram one day that I intended to corroborate her testimony about the high regard certain white folks downtown had had over many years for the residents of her street, Short Court. I made my announcement after the departure of an elderly employee of the gas company. (Gram has commented that he must have been coming to her home for sixty-some-odd years.) Gram was outraged: one, that I would consider going around behind her to check on stories; two, that I even had the idea of talking about her to somebody who operates gas meters. She was furious at this multilayered violation of our confidence in one another. At one level, I think she thought I thought she would lie. I argued back that scholarly historical work had to go by cross-checking of this kind. She didn't care about history, then. We fought that afternoon over what would and would not be part of my method. In more usual circumstances of doing research, penetration to this level of what is latent in the routine of interviewing most likely would not have come up.

In the end, I could not establish as "fact" that white folks downtown considered Short Court residents to be "aristocratic," in Gram's terms, although I certainly know from other contexts that white Charleston, for some intents and purposes, distinguished "respectable" black people from others. What our argument did establish is that Gram believed in, and perhaps was invested in, the special distinction, to white eyes, of the stratum to which she belonged. Was Gram remembering an aspiration or a fact? Later on that afternoon, her longtime friend Mrs. DaCosta dropped by to sit a spell on the porch, and Gram by skillful direction obtained corroboration from this dignified lady. (Not only that, we got quite a lot about special distinction of her own family. I should come over one day and learn more. . . .)

Fighting with my informant is a red light I ran on many afternoons. One of these fights was about what is or is not a relevant set of facts in an account of a public event—in Charleston—for presentation to a public much larger than Charleston's—the future readers of *Lemon Swamp and Other Places*. In this case, Gram did the cross-checking of memory, and it was I who rejected the process. The issue was what can be called the "wedding list" or the "church program" sort of memory.

This sort of memory has quite particular features: the utter necessity of getting it right; the methodological assumption of ordinary folks that any mistake is meaningful; a corresponding anxiety about forgetting on the part of the rememberer; the consequential nature of the result; and, last but not least, a god-awful exhaustiveness that can overwhelm all it touches. Everyone knows the gnawing fear that accompanies this kind of remembering. And I daresay as well, no one has not at one time or another upheld it—by drawing conclusions about omissions deemed incapable of being inadvertent, or, from the other side, by clenching jaws and making omissions with cold-blooded intent. The enforcement of flawless memory of this kind is in the nature of many kinds of sociability. It embodies what not only cannot but must not be remembered mistakenly. But when we shift to our historical mode in regard to memory, even memory aimed at answering historical questions that are clearly embedded in sociability, the wedding list/church program sort of memory is out of place, an encumbrance, and trivial. Such was the scene for a particularly passionate argument with Gram. Standards imposed by sociability battled with others. Decisions about the inclusion or exclusion of details were subject to different rules for the two of us.

Gram was a leader in establishing integrated public day care in Charleston. I put the story in the book's epilogue. The typescript I gave to Gram said that Charlestonians got together to care for the children of working mothers.

> Grandmother Fields will tell you, reeling off the names of Charlestonian places from which people came to help—"Holy Communion Episcopal, Zion Olivet Presbyterian, Plymouth Congregational, to name those in

> the neighborhood, then St. Phillip's and St. Michael's, which are South of Broad, over toward the Battery, and, of course, Centenary, Old Bethel, and Wesley Methodist." Her list goes on. And you know what? she will go on, reeling off the name of pastors who came forward (p. 243).

When Gram saw this, she got down to historical business. She checked with others in a position to know and added, added, added. My epilogue absolutely would not do. It needed to mention Mrs. So-and-So, of Such-and-Such Streets. It could not possibly be published without remembering Pastor This-and-That. Why, these are the people I have worked with for decades. They deserve the credit. These are the people who have been waiting to see my book, who put their names down to buy the first copies off the press. My rejoinder, that no one outside Charleston would care, did not count: the important audience was in Charleston. If the details got tedious to outsiders, well, we couldn't help that. Gram's purpose assigned those details to what cannot, nay, must not be remembered mistakenly. My purpose consigned them to just as obligatory forgetting.[3]

These details are of a category familiar to scholars who try to reconstruct Africa's history using oral tradition. Gram's church-program memory (or anyone's) is an instance of ideologically tainted memory summoned in view of present political purposes. Like that observed among African groups, it has the function of legitimizing and stabilizing a claim to some distinction. And part of its purpose is to perpetuate, by rendering it creditable to those concerned, a respectable consciousness of we-feeling. In that case memory "tainted" by interest is a dead-serious party to the creation of something true. The "mistakes" it may embody represent an imperfection only in light of the particular purposes scholarship has. Our scholarly effort to get the "real" past, not the true past required by a particular present, does not authorize us to disdain as simply mistaken this enormously consequential, creative, and everywhere visible operation of memory. It may be the case that human memory has it as a large-sized portion of its nature to be, in the psychologist Craig Barclay's splendid phrase, "true but not veridical."[4] Considerations of this sort carry us back to Nietzsche's identifying memory as a building block of sociability.

Returning again to our own opinions, however, we can take such considerations as a way of reminding ourselves of the biases scholarship requires us to adopt in our vocation to correct for bias in our data and to select what is "significant" in terms of a given research program. In our dealings with informants, we constantly look beyond the encounter toward a scientific horizon where what matters is literal facticity, veracity, representativeness, general applicability, relationship to a set of questions generated by theory, and above all, relevance in terms of scheme that designates what we need—and what we do not need—to know, what needs to be remembered and what is legitimately forgotten.

Although I did try to compromise, I did not make all my grandmother's amendments, which she crammed into the margins and which still spilled over onto extra pages—publishable remembering required their deliberate forgetting. On the other hand, I have kept them for our archive, well imagining some future historiographic predicament from which these names and places may provide a scholarly exit. Nonetheless, this action did not provide Gram an exit from her social predicament. It has troubled me ever since to reflect that preparing *Lemon Swamp* for publication required of me a certain condescension toward Gram and her compatriots.

This certain condescension was essentially no different from the systematic condescension toward the not-great with which we routinely tax documentary sources. I ask myself, now, how the church-list episode with Gram was different from what happened to my grandmother's Great-Great-Uncle Thomas, who she said accompanied his owner's sons as their valet, when they were sent to Oxford to have the rough edges knocked off their "aristocratic" South Carolina slaveholders' upbringing. Having been taught by those boys during slavery, Thomas educated his own and others' children, in a clandestine school—English, Latin, Greek, and Hebrew, according to Gram. In consequence, Thomas's children were among those well-educated freedmen whom the missionary churches recruited to be leaders. Face-to-face with a remarkable set of facts, and trained to mistrust such claims, I deputized a friend, off to Oxford for studies, to find out what he could about slaves resident in the colleges in the 1830s or thereabouts. The answer: records of who lived there 150 years ago were scarce; names of servants resident with them were nonexistent—because irrelevant. What would have been the conceivable purpose of remembering one "Tom," who laundered the shirts of Masters So-and-So and Such-and-Such Middleton? Those details held no more interest then than somebody else's church program list does for us now—or that Gram's list of Charleston luminaries in the day-care movement has. Only a then-unimaginable future historiography could make the names of slave servants resident at Oxford worth remembering. So while the contents of my grandmother's communication about her Great-Great-Uncle Tom are rich and suggestive about a number of issues, Gram's communication could not be transformed into information.

I did, however, take one more stab at transforming Gram's story about Thomas Middleton into information about Charleston's past. The source for most of the stories about dead Middleton kin had been Anna Eliza Izzard, whom everyone called Cousin Lala. Lala had graduated from Avery Institute, a private high school for freedmen established by the American Missionary Association, and then from Claflin University, established by the Methodist Church. (One of Thomas's sons, J. B. Middleton, was among those recruited to Claflin's first board of trustees.) After earning her B.A., Lala established a private school at her parents' home in Short Court. There she taught "black history," part of which was family history, including the saga of Thomas. Now, sometime in the 1920s a black doctoral student named T. Horace Fitchett had come to Charleston to collect oral testimony from local black people. Gram told me he collected a great deal from Lala. Thereafter he had taught for many years at Howard University. Reasoning that his notes and papers might yield corroboration, I contacted Howard's Moorland Collection, and through it, his widow. Mrs. Fitchett told me his papers would eventually be turned over but that tragic circumstances at present made my consulting them impossible. Thus ended for purposes of the book my attempt either to make of Gram's story a bit of information or to discredit it as that. The historical fact that neither could be done appears in the text as the naming of Gram's sources—mainly Lala and a less distinct figure called "Aunt Jane." Therewith I abandoned a would-be "fact" on the less respectable territory, so far as scholarship is concerned, of mere communication.

But then, not long ago, I happened to read an essay that made me think further about this respectable territory of verifiable fact: "The Storyteller," by Walter Benjamin.[5] In it he observes that the main form communication takes in the modern world is that of information, a form which, in his words, "lays claim to prompt verifiability." He goes on to characterize this development not as an advance but as an impoverishment. Storytelling dies, he says, as this new form of communication arises. Storytelling's successor, information, represents an impoverishment because, and to the degree that, the producer of information accomplishes precisely what we scholars strive to do: namely, to induce some body of material to deliver up explanation of its own accord, without our adding anything to it. "But the finest stories," according to Benjamin, "are characterized by the lack of explanation." Because the hearer or reader is left to interpret according to his own understanding, "the narrative achieves an amplitude that information lacks." If it involves our own participation, achieving this "amplitude that information lacks" is precisely what we as researchers strive not to do. Therefore while we seek narrative from our informants, we are specifically precluded from handling it in such a way that it remains what it was at birth.

According to Benjamin, it is the nature of every real story to contain "openly or covertly, something useful." And the utilities of stories include "counsel." "[C]ounsel," he goes on, "is less an answer to a question, than a proposal concerning the continuation of a story that is just unfolding. To seek this counsel one would first have to be able to tell the story. . . . Counsel woven into the fabric of real life is wisdom. The art of storytelling is reaching its end because the epic side of truth, wisdom, is dying out." Anyone who said in a conference on oral historical method that the researcher sought "wisdom" or "counsel" from his informants would, I believe, be met with stunned silence. We are usually free not to attend to these possible features of what we hear. But when we exercise this freedom to disregard an inborn feature of what we encounter, what does this do to memory contained in it? What have we done, and what have we foregone, by carrying out surgery so as to put "fact" in a specimen bottle while throwing the unexamined rest of the body into the disposal unit?

My own freedom from the constraints of scholarship went along with unfreedom in this regard. Since the project of doing *Lemon Swamp* did not change the relationship of grandmother and granddaughter, the elements of "wisdom" and "counsel" were not ignorable and hidden but explicit and obligatory. She was, after all, addressing the child of her child. Gram was didactic. My attempt to transform another of her communications into information, into something that laid claim to prompt verifiability, engendered another fight. In this case, the offending deed was to take a photograph of the Calhoun statue for inclusion in the book, offering readers thereby a kind of "proof" for an observation of Gram's, thus replicating the trip I made to see the object she referred to. Key points of the story were not verifiable, as I will now show. Let me start by quoting her on the subject of the statue of Senator John C. Calhoun, the indefatigable defender of slavery and states' rights.

> [W]e all hated all that Calhoun stood for. Our white city fathers wanted to keep what he stood for alive. So they named after him a street parallel to Broad—which, however, everybody kept on calling Boundary Street for a long time. And when I was a girl, they went further: they put up a life-size figure of John C. Calhoun preaching and stood it up on the Citadel Green, where it looked at you like another person in the park. Blacks took that statue personally. As you passed by, here was Calhoun looking you in the face and telling you, "Nigger, you may not be a slave, but I am back to see you stay in your place." The "niggers" didn't like it. Even the "nigger" children didn't like it. We used to carry something with us, if we knew we would be passing that way, in order to deface that statue—scratch up the coat, break the watch chain, try to knock off the nose—because he looked like he was telling you there was a place for "niggers" and "niggers" must stay there. Children and adults beat up John C. Calhoun so badly that the whites had to come back and put him up high, so we couldn't get to him. That's where he stands today, on a tall pedestal. He is so far away now until you can hardly tell what he looks like. (p. 57)

The point of that story, made repeatedly in many different ways, was that even during the ascendence of Jim Crow, even when it appeared from the outside that black people had capitulated to their defeat, they resisted; even the children resisted. The counsel was, You resist, too. Be a worthy descendent of Thomas and J. B. and Lala and the others. You do it, too. "You do it, too" is not something we researchers are prepared to take seriously from informants. Indeed, this aspect of the narratives we hear for our scholarly purpose raises a danger flag, marking bias, ideological special pleading, and the like. The flag marks a familiar site of misremembering, where the "should-have-been" displaces the "was," where wishes fill the blanks where facts are to be placed by dint of our own industry.

I proceeded with industry. I made myself conspicuous in the reading room of the Charleston Historical Society, depository of many documents pertaining to the past of a very historically conscious city. Conspicuous: because I, like other black people of Southern heritage, still do not enter such formerly segregated places unself-consciously or unnoticed. I spent two days searching for "information": I expected or hoped to learn that "rowdy" members of the "colored race" had vandalized this public work of art. Instead I learned something that prevented the facts from speaking for themselves, that pushed into a dead end my search for mere information. What I found out was much more interesting. It opened out instead of pinning down Gram's story.

It turns out that in 1854, the year Calhoun died, the Ladies' Calhoun Memorial Association began planning the memorial. In 1879, they were finally able to commission A. E. Harnisch of Philadelphia to execute a bronze statue of Calhoun on a Carolina granite pedestal, surrounded by allegorical figures—Truth, Justice, the Constitution, and History—at a cost of forty thousand dollars. But Harnisch in the end built the memorial with only one of the female figures—and she in such a state of disrobement that some of the ladies are said to have fainted at the unveiling. When the white folks recovered themselves sufficiently for straight thinking, they found historical fault with the clothing besides the aesthetic fault with the nakedness: Harnisch had put Calhoun into a Prince Albert coat, an anachronism. Black Charlestonians figured in the city-wide uproar in a curious way. The public work of art began to be called, in Gullah syntax, "Calhoun and he wife." A newspaper article says, "Because of the female figure's state of disattire, the nickname greatly distressed the ladies of Charleston and Mrs. Calhoun who was still alive."

Besides, the statue's construction was poor, the pose bad, and "his right index finger pointed in a different direction from the others, a habit peculiar to him in speeches, but in this instance exaggerated to the point of deformity." The various discomfitures continued until 1895, when the *Charleston Post* was able to report that "the old statue which has so long been a thorn in the flesh of the ladies of the Calhoun Monument Associa tion . . . to say nothing of the general public, will be taken down and con signed to oblivion." Massey Rhind of New York won the commission t execute Mr. Calhoun No. 2, erected in June 1896. No. 1 found his restin place in the Confederate Home Yard. A finger (it is not said which) wa placed in the Charleston Museum. There ends the story obtainable at th Charleston Historical Society.

There is no mention of the oddly tall pillar that stands on top of th grand, wide conventional pedestal with its luxuriating scrolls at the corner and its dignified plaques of speeches on each side. No explanation i offered for the remarkable disproportion of line that the pillar creates no for the fact that if you want to study Calhoun's features with your eye, o with that of a camera, you are interfered with by the sun and sky. Nothin I could find notices certain Charlestonians' notice of the statue beyon the raucous Negro laughter implied by the nickname "Calhoun and h wife."

Gram and I fought about the picture I took of the statue. Innocently, had intended it to illustrate her story. Gram said she would never have picture of "*that man*" in her book. She was still passionate about personage dead by then for nearly a century and a half. She intended, wit malice aforethought, to exclude him from the list of guests—just as surely as the ladies' society intended to include him on their own.

I have already devoted more time to topics regarding the color line than my grandmother would have approved of. I need to pause to say something about this fact. Gram would be the first to say that *Lemon Swamp* is about her own life: it is not about the racist system that partly enclosed it. Matters of race and color are a permanent presence without being her principal subject. They are constituent to life, but they do not define life. So, for example, Gram fondly remembers the details of her very fancy wedding—a black affair, from beginning to end—but yet notices that curious white people from the neighborhood slipped into Wesley Church's gallery silently to behold the occasion's splendor. On the other hand, when she decided to go to Boston to get her trousseau and took the Clyde Line Ship, she did not at first remember whether it was segregated. The point was the adventure. She did not pay attention to where white people were on the ship. And in her story of the time she collided with a car driven by a white man, the initial subject had been proper dress, the motto mothers and aunts of all colors tell their nieces and daughters, "Dress, you never know." It turned out that she had thrown a coat atop her nightgown on the day of that accident. Her Aunt Harriet, severe exponent of "Dress, you never know," was proved right (such women usually are!) as Grandmother made her way through downtown offices after the accident. But the fact that all the officials were white and all the aftermath nfolded downtown, among "downtown white folks," colors for her in a istinctive way a comeuppance anyone could have had. I would call these eatures "involuntary memory," if the term had not already been filched rom Proust and assigned a technical meaning. I use the term "unintended memory" instead, and I sometimes think it is also unintendable.

Even so, such features are often not the main subject of the story, from Gram's point of view. This point needs emphasizing because, as I continue xploring matters of race and color here, I acknowledge that these did not ommand Gram's front-burner attention as they do mine. They are there in he way Mount Kilimanjaro is there in Africa. For many intents and urposes, it is *merely* there, rising to its snow-capped peaks over the lux-riant topicality of the town of Moshi: it is hardly to be missed yet hardly o be noticed, at once native and alien to the life around it. Tourists are the nes who preoccupy themselves with looking at it. I am saying this to give varning that, as Gram's interlocutor, I was a tourist to her life with a ourist's habit of gawking. Gram criticized me more than once for my reoccupation. She called me "angry." Once she even called me "ugly" n the subject and asked, "What must those people be doing to you up here?" ("Up there" was Massachusetts at the time.) So I invite you to xercise methodological mistrust in my case, to be suspicious of the elections I have made in my own exercise of remembering. It is a fact that cannot help gazing at Kilimanjaro.

The Kilimanjaro I gaze at, not always uncovered by clouds and mist, often comes into view in the form of unintended or unintendable memory. The inner horizon of the South's racial order is not the aspect we generally end to think of first. It is easier to think of the South's Jim Crow regime in ts outward and visible signs—its laws, its segregated spaces, its economic rrangements, its intermittent physical atrocities, and its civic iconography, tems such as Calhoun's statue. But one learns through the testimony of nhabitants that it can at the same time be mapped out as an inward and nvisible topography. It has objects analogous to mountains, rivers, and the ike, which must be climbed, crossed, circumambulated, avoided, or otherwise taken into account. At the same time that these are not visible to he naked eye, and not immediately obvious to aliens on the scene, to nsiders, much of the time, they are not specifically noteworthy. They emain, in the phrase of Harold Garfinkel, "seen but unnoticed" features of social life.[6] As such, they enter human memory. They often emerge in oral estimony as unintended memory. In actual life they emerge above all as social order.

Whenever we start from a remove in time or space, these topographical features begin to seem less substantial than they are. We tend to think of them as movable by a mere movement of thought. Consider, for example, he seventeenth-century English revolutionaries whom Christopher Hill

describes in *The World Turned Upside Down.* These people embark o
militant political projects by shaking and quaking, talking in tongues, a
listening for the voice of prophecy. To us, they seem to be making a bizar
detour around a God present on the ground of ordinary experience th
we nevertheless cannot see. To us, it seems there are more practica
straight-ahead routes. It is as though we watch from above as huma
beings walk, as we might walk, across a flat heath. But, unlike us, they the
turn to walk around what seems to us a nonexistent obstacle. Of cour
the obstacle is really there, unavoidably and materially there; but th
knowledge of what it is, where it is, and *that* it is, they carry in memory.

The memory I am talking about is not the individual's own. It is instea
the fruit of a collaboration among the inhabitants of a common soci
locale. Having said this much, I think I can avoid the troubling yet ex
pressive term *collective memory*,[7] although I mean something like it. O
rather, I mean to say that fundamental features of human memory are no
grasped at the level of the isolated individual. Upbringing—or, to use m
discipline's term, socialization—provides the context in which the huma
brain's, and mind's, imperfect capacity for memory develops. It is also
process by which human beings acquire things that cannot be remembere
mistakenly. I want to present one example of this that emerged as unin
tended memory.

Last spring while I visited my grandmother, a middle-aged woma
dropped by. This woman and her brother had been Gram's pupils on Jame
Island. They started to reminisce about those school days over forty year
ago. After a time, Gram spoke about the brother. What a fine, bright pup
he had been over the years. And very cute as a little fellow: his mother ha
liked to dress him in outfits with Peter Pan collars. And, oh, he was smar
he had a grand future because of his mind. The conversation seemed to b
humming along in trivial sociability (generous recollections abou
someone's family being very good form), but then I heard my grandmothe
saying, What they did to him was such a tragedy. How they could tak
that fine young man and put him in jail for all those years! How it brok
the mother down! They both shook their heads in commiseration. M
antennae went up. When I finally got my question in between the head
shaking, the sister turned to me. Well, he didn't do it. The other boy did it
but he never would admit, *never would admit*, so all those years m
brother was in jail for what he did. He walked all around among us big a
day, year in, year out, may he rot . . . and so forth in that vein, the anger a
the other boy coming alive again, boiling, and engulfing the Englis
syntax. Well, what happened? What happened: He never did ask for no
drink of water, they said he sassed that white girl, talking about how he
want some water, my brother ain't do that, know better than that. Ain'
stop to ask that girl nothin'. That other boy did, and *my* brother went to

il, never would own up that *he* ask for that drink of water. My brother ent to jail in place of him. In a rush of renewed emotion, the woman had rived at an invisible mountain and begun to walk around it.

I piped up that neither one of them should have gone to jail twenty ears over the asking for a drink of water, not your brother and not the her boy either. If I hadn't seen the mountain yet, the awful way she oked up at me, and then ignored me, let me see it. I let further comment e in my mouth. I then saw what she saw, a black teenager who let his iend be convicted in his place. She did not see what I suddenly saw, a outhern tableau: the impressionable white girl and her oppressive male n (or perhaps the oppressive girl and her impressionable kin) enforcing unjust etiquette of domination. A black young man did not ask a white oung woman to address any sort of personal or bodily need. Her outrage the wrong injustice revealed the Jim Crow order with an immediacy that tentional testimony never could. For this kind of unintended memory, I ıbmit that cross-checking is redundant.

For those of us who try to glean from personal testimony the movement f history, as well as history's congealment in an order, what is interesting the end is the ferment. We want to glean from people's recollection hat territory remained unsubdued, perhaps unsubduable, by the Jim row regime's obligatory remembering. We want to find out when and ow they come to note, and wonder at, the positively audacious presence f Kilimanjaro. Not accidentally, it is in the domain of education that we nd continuous evidence of such ferment and continuous guerrilla war, for ducation is about what we agree that the young should carry in their inds: what schoolbook lessons and what nonschoolbook lessons they hould receive, about where they stand in the world and what that world made of. In the 1950s, when the issue was desegregation, the guerrilla attles to fill the mind differently made the transition to conventional arfare.

But in the 1920s and 1930s, Gram's heyday, this fight proceeded in the outh on a personal or local scale, underground, and hit and run. But I ould maintain that the larger fight that later entered national awareness is nconceivable without it. One recent Tuesday night, PBS's "MacNeil-ehrer News Hour" ended with one of its learned essays about national fe. Roger Rosenblatt invited us to contemplate how Dwight D. Eisen-ower, the "sleepy conservative" president, surprised those who had lected him, by "launching the civil rights era." His memory could not ave been more mistaken. The launching was done by the people whose usiness it was.

This launching was done not only by those who put their hand on the low, and their eyes on the prize, in the 1940s and 1950s, but also by thers who began long before that. Gram loved to tell the story of old Mrs.

Burden, who lived on the same James Island where black people i
thousand ways were inculcated with the unjust etiquette I described.
doubt in many of those ways Mrs. Burden was inculcated, too. But a
military widow, she was collecting a pension, which meant that she had
collect her check from the downtown white powers-that-be. When Gr
began to teach her pupils' parents and grandparents, Mrs. Burden made
her business, old as she was, to learn to sign her name. People asked h
why she bothered and asked Gram why she bothered with a pupil so o
But Mrs. Burden kept on coming and brought the teacher, Gram sa
"more eggs than the law allows." She was determined to be able to wa
into that office of downtown white folks one day and sign for her pensi
properly. Mrs. Burden was after a schoolbook lesson; she was after a no
schoolbook lesson. She was determined to stop having to put hers
down as "X." Gram said, "The day Mrs. Burden could go into that offi
and write 'Mrs. Samuel Burden,' she almost didn't need her walki
stick." In fights as small-scale and personal as this one—the fight to
known by one's own name—the guerrilla war went on in the worst
times, blasting away bit by bit the invisible mountains of the Jim Cro
South.

Let me close by saying that, during my time of liberation from scholar
constraint, Gram assigned me a part in a continuing guerrilla war in whi
memory is not only a source of information about the past but also a for
in creating the future. But, in a development that gave me many hours
methodological bad conscience, coming to grasp history in th
immediately human sense involved departing from rules that define its i
comparably paler counterpart, a mode of scientifically disciplined study.
the process, I had to think again about what this scientific discipline is fo
what a present-day scholar's pursuit of knowledge is and is not, and aft
thinking again, to see how called-for modesty is about what it can add
civilization. What does inquiry disciplined by the ideals of scienc
accomplish—if it is neither here nor there in terms of the growth of th
individual, if it must by its nature remain silent, as my mentor Max Web
says, on the question What shall we do, and how shall we live?, if it par
doxically says that one way we shall live, as researchers, is according to a
ethics of research that pertains to research and aught else, if it cuts throug
the flesh of human communication to expose for viewing an internal orga
but marvels not at the act of surgery, if it is passionately committed to
search for truth that is not, cannot, and must not be a quest for wisdom?

None of this is meant to disparage the scientific model of knowledg
but it is meant to take note of the possibility that the very prestige of thi
model in an Age of Information may obscure what is particular and od
about it and thus obscure what vital tasks this mode of pursuin
knowledge leaves undone, unconceived, perhaps even unconceivabl

ith this conundrum about method, I leave off speaking for myself and let e Polish poet Czeslaw Milosz say what I think I have come to nderstand.

> "To see" means not only to have before one's eyes. It may mean to preserve in memory. "To see and to describe" may also mean to reconstruct in imagination. A distance achieved thanks to the mystery of time must not change events, landscapes, human figures into a tangle of shadows growing paler and paler. On the contrary, it can show them in full light, so that every event, every date becomes expressive and persists as an eternal reminder of human depravity and human greatness. Those who are alive receive a mandate from those who are silent forever. They can fulfill their duties only by trying to reconstruct precisely things as they were, and by wrestling the past from fictions and legends.[8]

t is by trying to reconstruct things as they were by *all* means—those that artake in scientific method, and those that display the method's limits—hat we fulfill our historic duties and, at the same time, fulfill our uintessentially human desire to know with nourishment worthy of it.

Notes

1. Friedrich Nietzsche, "Second Essay. 'Guilt,' 'Bad Conscience,' and the Like," n *The Genealogy of Morals: A Polemic*, trans. Horace B. Samuel, Vol. 13, *The Complete Works of Friedrich Nietzsche*, ed. Oscar Levy (New York: Russell & Russell, 964), 59f.
2. Mamie Garvin Fields with Karen Fields, *Lemon Swamp and Other Places: A Carolina Memoir* (New York: The Free Press, 1983), xiii.
3. I note in this connection that it is very good form in church-program memory o thank people for effort they did not expend—yet.
4. Craig Barclay, "Truth and Accuracy in Autobiographical Memory," in *Practical Aspects of Memory: Current Research and Issues, Vol. I. Memory in Everyday Life*, ed. M. M. Gruneberg, P. E. Morris, and R. N. Sykes (New York: Academic Press, 1978).
5. Walter Benjamin, *Illuminations*, ed. Hannah Arendt, trans. Harry Zohn (New York: Harcourt, Brace & World, 1968), 83-109.
6. Harold Garfinkel, *Studies in Ethnomethodology* (Englewood Cliffs, N.J.: Prentice Hall, 1967).
7. I find this notion to be fascinatingly explored, in all its riches and some of its roublesomeness, in Bogumil Jewsiewicki, "Collective Memory and the Stakes of

Power: Reading of Popular Zairian Historical Discourses," *History in Africa* (1986): 195-223.

8. Czeslaw Milosz, *Nobel Lecture*, 8 December 1980 (Oslo, Norway: The No Foundation, 1981).

COMMENT

Alphine W. Jefferson *is a professor of history, black studies, and urban affai at the College of Wooster. Jefferson has focused his work in oral history on bla studies, most recently on blacks and Jews in Chicago. Here he draws on Fields essay to discuss the role of memory in establishing cultural—especially racial- identity.*

Karen Fields's paper is called "What One Cannot Remember Mistak enly." Being provocative, this title implies, as the paper states, that memor fails. In so doing, we are cautioned to remember that all oral document like written histories, are themselves enduring agreements, representing n what actually happened but what we—the interviewer, the interviewe and the larger culture—need to remember mistakenly. Let me say a wor here about sources. Although I was trained as a traditional historian, I hav always been suspicious of traditional historical sources. The written wor is said to be sacrosanct, immutable, and uncontaminated. Yet, I am als aware—and I caution you to be aware—that just as memory fails, so i there failure in the creation of those sources. The written word, whic traditional historians hold so dear, is not more unbiased or biased than an oral document we can create. We all walk around with a set of cultura presumptions and social assumptions which determine how we experienc the world, and thereby make judgments, including historical judgments. B way of reemphasis, let me say that memory fails and that humanity is frail Thus, all academic documents should be treated with equal skepticism an examined with rigor. I resent those who say that oral history is trendy an popular. It is, in actuality, the oldest form by which any culture remembers even if mistakenly, its collective past.

A few remarks about Professor Fields's book *Lemon Swamp* are i order here. She must be commended for such a brave undertaking. Fo though she claims to have liberated herself from the constraints of bein sociologist, historian, and granddaughter, all of those variables, as well a several other prominent ones, figure importantly in this work. As the grandmother told stories, Professor Fields, the sociologist, historian, and granddaughter—all gathered information. I am not suggesting that she is schizophrenic here—I'm simply saying that we filter information through what we are. A key to the presence of these variables is the regular argument she had with her informant and the dichotomous sense of what priorities would determine what information would go into the book. Her grandmother wanted things which were correct, proper, and even necessary information to tell this story the way she understood it, even if mistakenly. There is a major difference between the interests of the researcher and those of the informant. I simply say here that for all the objectivity Professor Fields claimed—like the rest of us, who also claim that—we cannot transcend our own demographic specifics; they are important forces and should be understood as such, informing any document, oral, visual, or written.

I am going to comment on a few things that sort of jumped out at me and demanded that I say something about them. The first is the condescension Professor Fields mentioned she feels toward her grandmother. I suggest she *had* to feel that, *needed* to feel that, in order to distance herself to create as objective a document as possible. This is an academic posture we all try to claim, we all seek to obtain; however, we seldom do so. History is not neutral. The writing of history or anything else is a self-conscious political act, and though we may seek objectivity in the interpretation of our sources, in so doing we are rendering the past in a certain fashion, whereas someone else would use the same material and render the past differently. Professor Fields is no exception here. We all carry around this condescension—for want of a better word, arrogance—so I came up with the phrase, "intensity of indifference." It is not easy to transcend the barriers of ethnicity, race, class, gender, and religious upbringing. An awareness of these crucial differences is especially important in oral research.

What leapt out at me very clearly was the story about her great-uncle who probably went to England to be a valet to the good Southern white boys. In her search to uncover material on this, she found nothing. However, the value of this search is that if such materials were available, they would be extremely important to us historically because these kinds of materials are not created with an historical self-consciousness. Thus we use them simply as the documents which are available to us. The story about oral information being passed on to give counsel is very important, and it is a very important part of black culture. Information is often given in a circumvented way, through tales and stories and fables and Biblical passages. I was always told by my mother that "pride goeth before destruction." She would never tell me that I was being prideful; she would

just simply quote that to me. Or they would always tell me I was alwa
looking up in the air, and I would never find money because I had my no
up in the air; I should look down on the ground. In this way, also, blac
people communicated, and historically have done so, information abo
how to succeed. One of the things that black females have always taug
their daughters was to "keep yourself up," "keep yourself up." That so
of meant keep your skirt down and be cool and don't do certain kinds
things. But they would never approach that taboo subject, the subject
sex directly, so they would say "keep yourself up" or "don't come hom
holding the bag," as one woman told me she was told. She came hom
pregnant, but she certainly wasn't holding the bag.

The point about Mount Kilimanjaro also jumped out at me. And I thin
it is instructive for the study of memory. If I may quote one of my poems,
think it summarizes it:

> I live in the world.
> I see it with these eyes.
> I feel it with this heart.
> I touch it with these hands.

For most of us, nothing is merely "there," as Fields cautions us. Everythin
informs our being, be it a mountain, an identity, or an experience. S
whether we are conscious of it or not, we are all seeing Kilimanjaro all o
the time.

That some black people are full of rage—Fields mentioned her grand
mother telling her that she was full of rage, and I can understand that—
should not be surprising to any of us, given the history of black people i
the country and the continued racism and discrimination. What is sad is th
fact that so few people recognize the source of this rage and continue t
perpetuate the very circumstances which create it. Obviously we all re
member mistakenly.

Karen Fields's paper reminds us that we often choose to remembe
mistakenly what we *need* to remember in order to preserve our individua
and collective identities.

RELIABILITY AND VALIDITY IN ORAL HISTORY: THE CASE FOR MEMORY

Alice M. Hoffman
Howard S. Hoffman

I.

lice M. Hoffman is Assistant to the Deputy Secretary for Labor and Industry for ;e State of Pennsylvania. A former professor of labor studies at Pennsylvania State 'niversity, she is a longtime advocate for the use of oral history research among ·orking-class Americans and in labor history research in general. The areas of her ;search interest and the quality of her work in academic and nonacademic settings ave distinguished Hoffman as an "oral historian's oral historian." She is past resident of the Oral History Association and has been an influential force in the evelopment of oral history in the United States. As coauthor and interviewer of .rchives of Memory: A Soldier Recalls World War II *(1991), she put to the test the oncept of oral history as a reliable research tool. In this paper she describes that emarkable project, where she tested the reliability of her husband's memory ırough corroboration with detailed official reports.*

It is an old business that we are about, even though oral historians and sychologists have been approaching the subject of memory directly only ather recently. For instance—oral historians always do this—we go back o Thucydides and to what he said in his introduction to the history of the 'eloponnesian War, "My conclusions have cost me some labour from the vant of coincidence between accounts of the same occurrences by differnt eyewitnesses, arising sometimes from imperfect memory, sometimes rom undue partiality for one side or the other."[1] Certainly since the 1960s, vhen oral history began to be preoccupied with definitions of itself, this ssue has been joined with a vengeance, in that the more traditional ıistorians have repeatedly said to us, How do you know that your nformants' memories are accurate? How do you know that they are apıropriate representations of the events they purport to describe? Now, for ı long time oral historians tended to respond, in the genre of "so's your nother," by pointing out that written documents are also suspect and that

oral documentation would simply have to be subjected to the traditio
canons of historical analysis as one would do with any other form of h
torical data.

At the 1967 National Colloquium on Oral History, Forrest Pogue, t
biographer of General George C. Marshall, described the combat intervi
program that was started by the army in 1943. In this project a team
army historians was assembled to interview soldiers just coming off t
line, tapping into a level of memory not dissimilar to that studied by Eli
abeth Loftus, who asks people about their memories fairly recently aft
presenting them with the material to be remembered. What was exciting
me about the army interview project was that it clearly made possible t
opportunity to examine in the archives of the history of World War
documents with an unusual immediacy, documents that would include t
perceptions of ordinary combat soldiers. At this same colloquium, howev
Cornelius Ryan, author of *The Longest Day*, the story of the D-D
invasion, offered some criticism of the interview process. He had read the
army combat interviews, and he also claims to have conducted s
thousand interviews of his own, and this is what he said about them:

> I discovered that interviewing is not reliable. I never found one m
> who landed on Omaha Beach who could tell me whether the water w
> hot or cold. I never found one man who landed on Omaha Beach wh
> could tell me the exact time when some incident occurred. . . . Gat
> ering the material after was very, very difficult indeed, and it did n
> lend itself to total accuracy.[2]

He went on to say, "In my kind of writing, one fact stands out mo
than any of the others—the very worthlessness of human testimony. U
less"—and he said he wanted to underline the word *unless*—"*unless*
can be substantiated by documents supporting the testimony."[3] Thus th
issue was joined, and it has occupied the discussions of oral historians an
their critics from that first colloquium until today.

Those two talks had a profound effect on my own thinking. They too
place in 1967, when I was very much a neophyte oral historian, hardl
knowing that that was what I was supposed to call myself. I was at th
time engaged in collecting the history of unionism in the metals industrie
I saw that this method would not only affect military history but lab
history as well, for now we had a technique that would enable us to re
cover and preserve not only the actions and attitudes of labor leadershi
but of the rank and file as well. I also recognized that accuracy of oral in
formants was an issue which we would have to address. Discussions abo
this with my psychologist husband, who was well schooled in th
scientific study of learning and memory, led me to break the question int

two parts. First, how reliable is human memory? Second, how valid is it? In this connection, reliability can be defined as the consistency with which an individual will tell the same story about the same event on a number of different occasions. Validity, on the other hand, refers to the degree of conformity between the reports of the event and the event itself as reported by other primary source material, such as documents, diaries, letters, or other oral reports.

My experience in conducting oral history interviews had led me to hypothesize that there might be a special character to the memories that we were tapping into. One such experience in particular was compelling. I had done an interview with a man named John Mullen, an employee of the Carnegie Illinois Steel Company in Clairton, Pennsylvania, at the time that unionism came into the metals industries. In my interview he described the means that had been used to attempt to recruit him to provide information for the company on the union activities of his fellow employees.[4] Some months later I found an anonymous interview in a book by Robert R. Brooks on the earliest attempts of steelworkers to organize.[5] Brooks published his book in 1940, yet this anonymous interview and mine were almost word for word the same! How could one account for this? I imagined that this was undoubtedly a story that Johnny Mullen had told and retold over the years until it had become extraordinarily well rehearsed. But when I questioned Mr. Mullen about this, he reported that, yes, he had had occasion to tell the story over the years, but at the time that I interviewed him it had been many years since he had given that particular incident much thought. I concluded, therefore, that this particular memory had remarkable stability and that it was remarkably reliable from youth into old age. I was aware, however, that when compared to other testimony and documents on industrial espionage, such as that uncovered by the Senate committee to investigate the violation of civil liberties, that there were slight discrepancies between his testimony and the preponderance of other available sources. Thus, while the information was reliable to a remarkable degree, its validity was somewhat less impressive.

In recognizing that the processes of human memory were basic to our methodology, oral historians over the years have, mistakenly in my view, invited psychiatrists and psychoanalysts to their colloquia. Yet this has not proven to be very fruitful because the psychiatrists and psychoanalysts that we have invited have been inclined to give rather anecdotal information. I think that the experimental analysis of the processes of memory has more typically been carried out by cognitive psychologists. In an effort to correct this situation, Howard and I devised a plan to examine the issue of memory utilizing the combined methodologies of psychological and historical analysis. In the conception of this study we were influenced by Forrest Pogue's description of the army combat interviews. However, it is important to recognize that we were preparing examine a much more long-term, autobiographical memory than wa typical of Pogue's after-action interviews.

The plan we came up with was that Howard would serve as an oral his tory interviewee and I would query him on his memory of his experience as a mortar crewman in World War II. I would conduct those interviews and I would also attempt to locate whatever official records might b available either to corroborate or disprove the stories that Howard woul tell. We carried out the interviews in three phases. First, we conducted set of interviews based on free recall in which we recorded on tape an transcribed the memories elicited simply by asking, "Tell me about th war." Questions were asked only to clarify or expand upon the informa tion provided. We selected this particular methodology because w wanted to avoid as much as possible influencing the memories by th questions that were posed. Some years later we repeated this process. I the intervening years Howard tried to avoid situations that might stimulat him to rehearse or further explore memories of his war experiences. H avoided war films and books and went about his business of teaching an research, activities which offered little occasion for him to think about, le alone discuss, his term as a soldier. The second recall document woul provide a test of the reliability of the original memory store. Finally, w conducted a third set of interviews which were based on wha documentary evidence could be located.

The first set of recall interviews was conducted in 1978. In that sam year John Neuenschwander published an article in the *Oral History Re view* entitled "Remembrance of Things Past: Oral Historians and Long Term Memory" in which, for the first time as far as I am aware, an ora historian looked at studies done by experimental psychologists. He con cluded his paper by making the following plea:

> Oral historians can and must begin to seriously study long-term mem ory. What is needed are studies of how interviewee memory claims differ over time. Reinterviewing narrators after five, ten, and fifteen-year intervals may provide helpful insights on long-term memory. . . Oral historians should also build into their interview format questions about memory. Explanations of how interviewees think their memories work could prove helpful.[6]

We were intrigued by Neuenschwander's article because it suggested that our approach might meet a need.

The second recall session that we conducted was done in 1982, little more than four years after the first. Meanwhile, I was fortunate to find that a careful and detailed record existed of the daily activities of Howard's company—Company C, Third Chemical Mortar Battalion—at the army archives in Suitland, Maryland. In addition to an account of the battle statistics for Company C, this record contained a daily log of activities in which Howard was engaged for the entire time that he was overseas. There were notations in this document which enabled me to know whether Howard had had a hot breakfast on a particular day. There were notations that drew maps that showed me exactly where the foxholes in which he slept had been dug. Thus it became possible to compare the free-recall interviews with this log and to conduct then a third set of interviews which we labeled validity documents.

In the third set of interviews we also used, in addition to the log, photographs taken by the U.S. Army Signal Corps, secondary sources, and cartoons, as well as photographs taken by the subject himself with a "liberated" German camera. In addition, we made a trip to Edgewood Arsenal, Maryland, where Howard had served in 1943 as a subject in some poison gas experiments. This made it possible to test Howard's memory claim about his experiences in these experiments, and it enabled us to determine how his memories might be affected by a return to the scene where some of the events had taken place. I was careful not to expose Howard indiscriminately to these sources. I showed them to him systematically and interviewed him subsequent to each exposure.

In the course of this research we discovered that the Third Chemical Battalion had been holding periodic reunions. We hadn't previously known of these meetings, but at the very end of the project we contacted the group and met with a few of these veterans near York, Pennsylvania. We later met with the entire reunion group at their biannual convention in Baltimore in July 1986. We recorded several interviews at these meetings and then recorded Howard's reactions to the meetings. We used all of these documents to examine our questions about the memory process.

What kinds of things did we find? The transcription of the first recall interview yielded a document of 140 pages. The transcription of the second recall interview was 142 pages long. His description of his induction into the army in both interviews was eleven pages. On the other hand, his description of being in the replacement depot prior to being sent overseas was one paragraph in each of the two interviews. While the number of pages devoted to each episode of the stateside experience was the same, the actual time that Howard spent in a given episode versus the space his memory devoted to it is uneven. For example, Howard was in the replacement depot prior to being sent overseas for at least three to four weeks. That episode merits one paragraph in both recall documents while the four weeks of the induction process prior to his arrival at boot camp in Alabama covers eleven pages in both documents.

What is illustrated in those cases is something that continues to be exhibited throughout the entire series of documents: a very strong primacy effect. The first time things are done, the first time an experience is recounted, it is remembered and recounted in much greater detail. For example, when he describes the wounding of a soldier on the liberty ship in route to Italy and his subsequent transfer to another ship in the convoy there is no incident which appears in the first interview which is not contained in the second. While the stories are not word-for-word the same and while the information is presented in slightly different sequence, the two versions are essentially the same. There are, however, interesting discrepancies of detail. In Interview One, twenty-one men are reported wounded by a shell burst; in Interview Two, five or six guys are wounded. In Interview One, Howard says that nobody even told them what had happened, but in Interview Two, Howard remembers talking to one of the men who "had some shrapnel somewhere." Aside from these details the narratives, especially as they relate to Howard's direct experience, are exactly similar.

These narratives are so similar that in both interviews the same hesitation is experienced at the same point in the account. In Interview One Howard starts to describe bringing the doctor from a destroyer to treat the wounded men. Then he starts to visualize the scene, has trouble with it, and says, "Well, let me think about this. They made two transfers at sea." He then proceeds to describe a scene in very visual terms. In the second interview at the same point in the narrative where he is describing the transfer, he stops again and says, "No, that isn't what happened. They put a boat out," and again what follows is a very detailed imaging of the description of the sailor in the boat. It is almost as if the image of the sailor in the boat interrupts and corrects the verbal narrative. In fact, there is much evidence to suggest that Howard's memories, unlike Johnny Mullen's, consist of a number of stored scenes. What Mullen had was a stored tape recording of the exact words to describe the event. What Howard has is a series of visualizations linked together by verbal construction to maintain the thread or the chronology of the narrative. In this regard it is interesting to observe that what is stored contains the basis for the interruption as well as the story.

Howard was first engaged in combat in Italy. He arrived at the front in early May and found himself attached to Company C, Third Chemical Mortar Battalion. The company had been fighting together since the African campaign. From their stories of the previous winter before Cassino, he understood that now he was to be part of the major spring offensive. He was impressed by the synchronization of the artillery bombardment which began the offensive. While he remembered the zero hour as eleven o'clock, he mistakenly placed it in the morning, when in fact it began at leven p.m. He did remember moving the ammunition up to the mortars in he darkness, and this memory is corroborated in a book by W. G. F. ackson called *The Battle for Rome*, in which Jackson describes the men noving forward in the dark:

> At eleven o'clock . . . the combined artillery of the Fifth and Eighth Armies opened fire. . . . The flashes lit up the black shapes of the mountains from Minturno on the coast to Monte Cifalco north of Cassino. . . . Juin's Frenchmen started their assault within minutes of the beginning of the artillery programme.[7]

Howard's memories of the event from the second set of interviews are as follows:

> *Alice Hoffman:* When did you first get into combat?
> *Howard Hoffman:* May 11, I think was the day. At eleven o'clock in the morning on the eleventh day of May, somehow is what I remember. At Castleforte was the first place that I experienced any combat. And they brought us up to Castleforte in trucks, and we unloaded hundreds and hundreds of rounds of ammunition, carried it up the mountainside to a place, sort of a quarter of the way up the mountain, set up the guns, and then we were told that we were to start firing at a particular time. Now, I think that we had set up the guns the day before, and it was the next morning that we were to start firing. And the officer was there with a stopwatch, and he told us when to exactly drop the shells in. And the interesting thing is that just before we fired I could see the guns behind us firing. That is, here are the guns way, way back like the long toms, the 240-millimeter cannons which could fire from miles. The impression I got was that they had tried to time things so that all the shells would land at the same time. Even though the ones farther away would fire sooner. That was the opening of my first experience of combat. [second recall interview]

In the first interview Howard had emphasized how heavy the mortar was and how many men it took to lug it up the steep hillside. He says, "I remember carrying it at night and in the daytime." He again emphasized the synchronization. But interestingly enough, when he described the hour at which the firing began, he qualified it in both interviews with the phrases "It seems to me like it was eleven o'clock in the morning" and "I think it was the next morning when we began to fire." In both interviews he emphasized the massive character of the bombardment. Historians, incidentally, have described this particular bombardment as rivaled only by the barrage at El Alamein in the annals of all war.

In the first interview, in response to the question, "Who was your commander?" Howard replied that he didn't know but that he thought his name was Captain Cook. He did remember, however, that he was young, blond, a stable leader, and from Louisiana. In the second interview, in response to the same question, he again states that he does not know, but

> We had somebody who—I keep thinking his name was Cooper, and I think he was from Louisiana, and he was a fairly young man, a captain. But I remember him from much later, from during the Bulge. In fact, it was during the Bulge that he was sent home on a furlough and came back again. And the name Cooper—and I'm not sure it's Cooper, because Frank Cooper was head of the Haskins lab, and I may have the names mixed up, but somehow the name Cooper seems appropriate. [second recall interview]

So note, this time he changes the name to Cooper. But he senses that this may not be correct, and he volunteers that Frank Cooper was also a much-respected authority figure from a later period in his life. He also now remembers more about the captain from the Battle of the Bulge.

When we searched through the records of Company C we found that the captain was named John Moore, that he was much admired by his troops, and that he was from Louisiana. Further, in September of 1985, after our research at the War College in Carlisle, Pennsylvania, had disclosed that the Third Chemical Battalion held these occasional reunions, we attended our first of these gatherings in York at the home of former Corporal Ralph Worley. While Captain Moore was unable to attend this particular meeting, he called from Louisiana and talked to each of the veterans at the reunion. That conversation caused Howard to remember that this officer had shared his liquor with his men on at least one occasion, an act of generosity remembered because it was extremely unusual. Now Captain Moore was brought back to what might be described as his rightful place in Howard's memory. Thus, we can conclude that these memories which seemed to be unavailable can be reintegrated given the appropriate stimulus.

These events also provide some evidence for the hypothesis that memories are not only chained but also cataloged under certain headings. For example, in the first instance, where Howard attempted to retrieve the name, he said "Cook," possibly because it is chained to Captain Hook in the Peter Pan and Wendy story. Further, since Howard's self-perception about his memory is that he cannot remember names, he doesn't search very hard for names, figuring, I think, that the effort won't be worth his while. In the second interview when he was asked the same question, he did engage in a more rigorous search and retrieved the name of Frank

Cooper. It is as if he has a subject file in his memory labeled "Respected Authority Figures," and while he has sensed that this was not correct—and even offered the explanation himself as to why this name emerged—he still was unable to produce the correct name. However, when we found the correct name in the records, he recognized it instantly and further, when he spoke to the man on the phone, a series of memories and stories about him emerged which were linked to his name and the conversations with him, some of which had previously been inaccessible. This suggests that there is information and experience in memory storehouse which, at any particular time that it is called for, may not be available but is not necessarily erased. However, this is not to say that all experience is retained but merely to suggest that more experience is retained than can be elicited by mere free recall and that more may be retrieved given appropriate cues.

The memories of the Italian campaign can be submitted to a rigorous validity analysis because events of the Italian campaign have been the focus of a great deal of historical interest. Howard's descriptions of the terrain can be verified in many other accounts and in photographs. The fact that he was fighting with the Free French Forces of General Juin and that these troops opened the road to Rome is all a matter of record. Furthermore, in the narrative it has now become possible to compare and contrast Howard's memories with the diary of events kept in the company headquarters on a daily basis. These entries corroborate much of Howard's memory but, of course, for many of his stories they offer no information at all. They are unemotional and, interestingly enough, sometimes designed to put the best interpretation on actions of the officers as is possible. The entry from the tenth of May will perhaps illustrate their character:

> The Company spent the day in preparation for the move to the forward area. The Company departed from battalion bivouac area at 2100B hours. There was much traffic on the road. The last truck was unloaded at the gun positions at 02030B hours, May 11th. The night was quiet and no enemy shelling. Casualties: None.[8]

Throughout the month of May these records corroborate Howard's memory of moving, setting up the guns, and moving again. In fact, they serve to explain that memory by commenting that "the Jerries were on the run and it was almost difficult to keep up with them." On the nineteenth of May the following incident is recorded in the diary:

> The Co. was awakened at 0520B by a heavy enemy shell burst close by that sounded like a delayed action bomb. Several men called for help about 20 feet away. Sgt Edmondson was lying with a lump of dirt

> the size of a bedroll on his chest and with a cut on his face. Capt Moore found no severe cuts on him, so ran to the other calls, and found Pvts Ryan and McGrady, the two first aid men, and Pvts DePresco and Childress buried in their slit trenches with only their heads exposed. Sgt Toscano's squad was summoned for help, and the two First Aid men were soon on their feet and uninjured. Pvts DePresco and Childress, however, were deeply buried and Pvt Aciz worked some 15 or 20 minutes digging them out. Pvt Childress was lifted onto a stretcher, but Pvt DePresco, who was underneath and somewhat protected, scrambled out and onto his feet. Sgt Edmondson, Pvts Childress and DePresco were sent back to BN Forward Aid Station. [Daily Log, 19 May 1944]

Now, this is the same story that was recounted by Howard in both interviews, and while it provides considerable corroboration, it also reveals some discrepancies. In the first interview Howard had described moving up to a small Italian cemetery where he slept one night with several other guys, and not finding it too comfortable, the next night he went to where the trucks were parked and dug a foxhole in a drainage ditch. In the morning he was awakened by an officer telling him that he was needed to help dig out some bodies. They dug furiously and pulled one guy out, another managed to free himself, but the one in the middle—which would have taken the direct hit—could not be found. Now, the one in the middle is not mentioned in the diary at all, but only in Howard's two recall documents. Later, the guy who was supposed to be sleeping in the foxhole in the middle came down the hill from where he had gone to sleep in a German dugout. So the middle foxhole had, in fact, been unoccupied.

In the second interview Howard said that he did not sleep in the cemetery. He remembered lying down in the crypt but found it eerie and uncomfortable, so he went below and dug into a ditch. He tells the same story about being awakened in the morning to dig the men out. He states that there were four men buried in their slit trenches, which is corroborated by the company history which names the four men. He again repeats the story about looking for the guy in the middle foxhole, not being able to find any part of him, and later seeing him come wandering into the breakfast chow line, much to Howard's amazement. The company history makes it clear that the second interview is the correct one with respect to whether or not he slept in the cemetery since they were not in this area for two nights, only one. The second interview also contains a more obvious effort to get the memory right and in so doing provides a very interesting insight into the memory process:

> We started digging mostly with our hands and we dug up, as I remember, four guys, and not one of them was hurt. Now, I can't picture it anymore; I seemed to think that last time I was able to say that I, you know, helped them up. But now I am not able to picture reaching down and grabbing them. . . . They had been buried alive but loosely by the dirt—but now I can't picture it anymore. That's the memory that's. . . . I can remember sort of standing there, I can remember. . . . I seem to think I have a shovel in my hand. I seem to think I'm pulling, but I can't picture lifting somebody up, coming across a person. The other thing is that the story—I can remember telling the story from four years ago and I remember. . . . This is what I remember about it, that the shell landed; it had just missed the truck coming in. If it had hit the truck which was loaded with ammo, we'd all be dead. It just missed the truck and landed in the middle foxhole. And the concussion apparently went up above all the other guys and covered them without killing them. Now, maybe they had been removed from the hole before I came along, but I remember the lieutenant telling, I do remember him physically waking me and saying that I had to come along and help dig these guys out. And the one who was in the middle, we couldn't find anything. And I remember digging and looking and there was no trace of him. And we assumed that he had just [been] completely disintegrated by the shell. Well, about an hour or two later, he comes walking down the hill. [second recall interview]

You can see the difference in the character of the two kinds of documents, the company diary and Howard's interview. There is a lot more emotion, a lot more subjectivity to Howard's description than there is in the diary. In the first interview, he had stated that after digging one guy out, before they could get to the next one, he saw earth moving and one guy managed to free himself. That apparently was a powerful image, because even in the rather dry account of the company diary it says this: "Pvt Childress was lifted onto a stretcher, but Pvt DePresco, who was underneath and somewhat protected, scrambled out and on his feet."

For whatever reason, there seems to have been a greater effort toward accuracy in the second interview than in the first, at least at this point in the narrative. The story about sleeping in the cemetery was one that had been told over the years to entertain friends. Presumably, actually sleeping there was judged by the narrator to be more interesting and entertaining than just thinking about sleeping in the cemetery. However, in the second interview, where he makes a strong effort to be accurate, he relies on an effort to call up the past, to image it in his mind's eye, and then to describe the image seen. In the effort to do this he draws several blanks and then becomes unsure about what, in fact, happened. What is clear, however, is

that we have here an event witnessed by Howard which is corroborate
by the archival record. Moreover, the effort to recover the incident reveal
interesting information about the basic strategies employed by Howar
when he makes an effort to provide accurate information from memory. H
tends to do so by calling up the image and then describing it.

Elizabeth Loftus and other researchers in the field of memory have de
scribed two kinds of rememberers, *verbal* and *image makers*. We see tha
Howard falls quite definitely into the latter category, which is perhap
consistent with his effort to become a professional artist later in life an
with the fact that throughout his life he has been interested in drawing an
painting and conveying his perceptions of the world by reproducing then
visually. Of course, we can't know how much error, distortion, and/o
corroboration there may be in stories told by Howard which are neither i
the company history, in other historical treatments of the Italian campaign
nor corroborated by information from other veterans in the same unit. Bu
on the basis of what can be validated, one can feel confident that these
stories at least contain a central core of fact, even though certain details are
missing or reconstructed in order to make sense of the memory as the effor
is made to share it with others.

Another characteristic of rememberers who rely on images rather thar
verbally stored scenes seems to be that they tend to place more confidence
in their memories than those who rely on verbal stories. After all, they are
simply calling up the scene and describing it; therefore, this has got to be
the way it is, right? If you cannot recall an event, there is a strong tendency on the part of visual rememberers to feel that it could not have happened. This characteristic is illustrated by the description of what took
place while Third Chemical was bivouacked on the Italian coast after
Rome had been taken and while preparations were being made for the invasion of southern France, known as Operation Anvil. During those
preparations, the company engaged in target practice by firing the mortars
out into the Mediterranean. Howard described an event during this practice when something ignited the nitrocellulose rings on the ammunition
and caused a flash fire which burned five or six guys very badly. Ralph
Worley also remembered this incident and described it even more vividly
than Howard. He said, "One guy just had the flesh hanging off his chest in
strings like hot cheese." Worley went on to say that Howard had gone out
in an amphibious vehicle to drag a target out into the sea. Howard did not
believe that this could have happened. He felt that he would have had a
great interest in such a vehicle and could not possibly forget having ridden
in one. We taped the following exchange between Ralph Worley and
Howard at the reunion in September of 1985:

> *Worley:* Well, I know you were there because I have a picture of you on that amphibious vehicle coming in. You went out with—
> *Hoffman:* I don't believe I did!
> *Worley:* I know you did! Because I have a picture of you coming back.
> *Hoffman:* You've got to show it to me! I've got to see that one.
> *Worley:* It was Lieutenant Meshany and our warrant officer and you and I believe Z. J. Hatcher, it might have been.
> *Hoffman:* Well, if it's a picture of me, it will be the first thing that's clear that's happened to me that I don't remember.
> *Worley:* They made a raft out of wood and then they put some kind of cloth on it and they took it out and set it out there and then they fired mortars at the target out on the Mediterranean and you were on the vehicle, one of those like a truck that you can go on land or sea.
> *Hoffman:* I've got to see this picture because I don't remember.
> *Worley:* Yeah! I have it in there. I'll show it to you. I've got a color slide.[9]

When the slide was shown, Howard still felt that it was not him, even though there was a chorus from the veterans who had known him of "That's you all right, Hoffman." Howard went close up to the picture, denying all the way that it was in fact a picture of him, until he saw a ring on the finger that he knew to have been his ring and that he subsequently had given to a French girl! But even after he was forced to acknowledge that this was indeed a picture of himself, and hence a valid experience from his own past, he was unable to remember the event and since the reunion he has continued to have no memory of the event. While he knows intellectually that it is not so, he feels that his picture is unrelated to his own experience.

How can this phenomenon be accounted for? Is this the only example of repression that we have found in this study? There is some evidence that this might be the case. In the first interview, as he begins to describe the events which took place when they were bivouacked on the beach, he says, "I also remember doing some target practice there—not target practice, shooting." Thus, there is a slight denial of the target practice. In the second interview, when he reaches the same point in the narration he says, "There are several incidents on the beach I ought to tell you about, but I can do it later though." I suggested that, no, we were almost through the story of the Italian campaign, so why not continue through to the end of that chapter? At this point he gave a big sigh and proceeded with the story of the flash fire.

There are also other reasons to reject the notion of repression. For one thing, it is difficult to hypothesize repression with absence of any reason for it. It is not the story of the fire that he doesn't remember, it is rather the story of what looks like a rather pleasant interlude out in a boat. On theory about memory is that it requires rehearsal in order to go into long term store. In this case it may be that the horror of the fire and his subse quent preoccupation with the fears attendant on making an invasion int southern France prevented the rehearsal of this event in the amphibiou vehicle. Whatever the cause of Howard's inability to remember the ride i the amphibious vehicle, one thing about it seems certain: it is absolutel unavailable for retrieval even with the most cogent of cues, namely, picture of himself in the vehicle at sea.

In the interviews which describe the fighting from southern France t the Elbe River in Germany, it is not so simple to make a judgment wit respect to the reliability of Howard's recollection, because in the secon recall document it was decided to force the story out of its chronologica sequence in order to ascertain what effect that might have on the memory process. After the description of the invasion I asked Howard to discuss the events associated with meeting the Russians at the Elbe River, which is obviously going clear to the end of the war. I said, "All right, let's star with reaching the Elbe River." His response: Long pause, "Well," he said "I have to back up a little bit, because you see—" long pause—"Well you see, I saw the Elbe River—we have some photographs of that. Now— I have to back up, and I don't know how far back to go. There are two incidents just prior to the end of fighting." Then he goes on to those previous incidents. His reaction, therefore, to going out of sequence indicates that his memory for the events of the war are at least partially strung together in a time line. Disturbing that organization resulted in considerable confusion for him. For much of the second recall document he described a series of incidents but was frequently confused as to whether they took place in France or in Germany. This was not usually the case in the first recall document. In the second recall document, after describing an incident, Howard would frequently, almost plaintively, say, "Do you want me to go on now from there to the end of the war?"

Forcing the narrative out of sequence resulted in a loss of material. That is, there is material which is in the first recall document which does not initially appear in the second. For instance, Howard had been assigned guard duty one night. At one point he heard strange noises coming from a parked jeep and called the password. When the counter sign was not returned he fired at the jeep. The noise turned out to be rabbits in a box. This has always been labeled "The Incident in which Howard Saved the Company from an Attack of Rabbits." This story was not recounted in the second interview until he was provided an appropriate cue:

Howard Hoffman: Alice assures me that there are gaps in what I recall. I suggest we ought to see what conditions might bring some of it back.

She says that a single word may be an adequate cue to reconstruct one story that is in the first document but not in the second. I'm challenging her to say that word.
Alice Hoffman: Rabbit.
Howard Hoffman: Oh, for goodness sakes, yes.

And he proceeded to tell virtually the exact same story that appeared in the first recall document. He was able in this fashion to recreate all of the missing stories from the first recall document when he was given appropriate cues. Thus, disrupting the organization of the encoding and memory seems to have confused the narrative, causing gaps, omissions, and confusions. But there seems to be a subset of organization, so that each incident as it is narrated remains intact and can be recalled in the same way whether it is freely recalled or cued.

In order to study the validity of Howard's memories of the fighting in France and Germany, we used a variety of strategies similar to those employed with the memories of the Italian campaign. Howard did not remember the exact date on which they made the invasion of southern France. But his memory that they went in a British ship and that they splashed ashore without casualties is confirmed in the daily log. There is, however, one element of actual disparity between the log and the recall documents—and this, by the way, is the only actual disparity that we found, but it is pretty severe. Usually the differences between the two documents are in regard to descriptions of events which Howard either did not experience or does not remember or, conversely, there are events which Howard recalled but which are not reflected in the log. But the following is an account where Howard's memory is actually at variance with the log.

At one time Howard's battalion bivouacked near a French town, Briançon, close to the border with Italy and Switzerland. Suddenly, the entire battalion came under such heavy enemy fire that they were forced to retreat into the mountains. When the shelling started, Lieutenant Jones was ordered to form a patrol and to determine where the firing was coming from. When the patrol returned they discovered that the entire battalion was gone. As recorded in the log, poor Lieutenant Jones and his men wandered around for several days and eventually, on September 3, were reunited with their company. Howard describes in his documents the departure of this patrol in graphic terms. He recalled watching them leave and begin to climb up the mountain, and when he described the incident he stated that he never saw them again. He thought he might have heard that they were captured by the Germans. In the second recall document the incident is described in the same way:

> I also remember, when this thing happened, they sent a patrol up into the mountains to go up and see what the hell was going on. I almost was on that patrol. But the guys who went on that patrol were never seen again. And I heard that they had been captured and spent the rest of the war in German prison camps. [second recall interview]

How can we account for his memory failure? It must be seen as a failure because there is in this log a detailed account of Lieutenant Jones's return. Furthermore, one of the enlisted men who was lost with Lieutenant Jones was Corporal Worley, who was Howard's friend, often in his squad, the photographer of the picture just discussed. How could Howard have failed to register the return of this friend? I believe one clue is in the research of Elizabeth Loftus. Her discovery that false information has a powerful influence on reports, and all the more so if the false information was supplied by an authority figure, is relevant here. I asked Howard to try to picture where he might have been when he was told that the patrol had been captured. He said that he thinks he was in a jeep with an officer. Another possible explanation is one that we examined before, namely, that some other preoccupation prevented the rehearsal and subsequent long-term store. Right after this incident Howard had a very good friend who was shot and killed in a rifle inspection, and he spent a good bit of time thinking about how terrible it was to lose your life in such a random and almost prosaic event.

There is another interesting possibility and that is, when Howard saw the patrol leave, he was so sure that they would be captured or killed that their disappearance became a self-fulfilled prophecy, so profoundly affecting his mental state that he did not process their return in his memory of events. This hypothesis is a kind of addendum to explanations provided by Loftus, and what we see here is the possibility that one's *internal* directions or observations may also affect memory in a similar fashion.

As was characteristic of the memories of the fighting in Italy, Howard does not report the events after the invasion of France and Germany in great detail. Thus, we see that even events of life-threatening character, if they are sufficiently repetitive, can be lost to memory. Once Howard's memories became episodic in nature, the number of time confusions became more frequent, even in the first recall document. "We were in the Vosges Mountains and I remember hearing about Roosevelt's death in a field on the edge of a woods." Howard was certainly in the Vosges Mountains in November but, of course, Roosevelt died on April 12, when they were in Germany. The confusion may have arisen from the fact that while in the Vosges Mountains, Howard undoubtedly heard that FDR had been reelected. After February 1945, it became more difficult to compare Howard's memories with the events cited in the daily log. For one thing the log itself tends to become less discursive. I have developed the hypothesis that this is now a different author of the log. It looks very much that way. And this portion of the log makes no mention of the atrocities Howard describes at Gardelegen in Germany. In 1978 Howard and I visited Yad Vashem, the memorial to victims of the Holocaust in Israel. Howard stopped short in front of a photograph depicting the atrocity at Gardelegen. It was labeled, "Gardelegen, a concentration camp in which [illegible]50 inmates were killed." In Howard's memory this was incorrect. What the picture depicted was a barn where the Nazis had herded about a thousand political prisoners that they had been marching to Hannover. But when they got word that Hannover had fallen, rather than let these prisoners go, they set fire to the barn and systematically shot any man who managed to claw his way out of the structure. When we returned to the U.S. we searched for some documentary evidence to confirm Howard's memory and found it in *Life* magazine for May 19, 1945. This is a picture taken by Margaret Bourke-White of Gardelegen, and the caption in the *Life* magazine states, "At Gardelegen, Friday, April 13, German guards incinerated a thousand prisoners to prevent their being liberated by advancing allied forces." We sent this information to Yad Vashem, and presumably the oral memory will correct the documents in that museum to the Holocaust.

Howard described Gardelegen like this:

> There were bodies that were just burned terribly. Some of them had on striped clothes, as I recall. I may be making that up about the striped clothes. That's what I'd seen in movies and stuff. But these guys didn't. [second recall interview]

This appears to be an interesting illustration of the reconstructive nature of memory. In the second interview, the victims are initially described as having striped clothes, but because Howard's primary strategy in recall is to visualize the scene as he called it up in his mind's eye, he saw that they did not have on striped clothes. He recognized his own error as a bit of reconstruction.

Having established that, with the exception of certain time confusions, the essential elements in Howard's memory of the battles in France and Germany are corroborated by either the daily log or by reference to some other primary resource, we now attempted to discover to what extent supplying him with recognition items from the log might call forth new memories. It didn't. We reviewed the daily log, which Howard was seeing for the first time. He recognized things from the daily log, and said, "Oh, yes," but no additional memories were stimulated. The same thing was true with our efforts to show him pictures from *Life Goes to War* and the pictorial record from the adjutant general's office. He would recognize the pictures and say, "Yes, that's what it looked like." But in only one very minor incident did it bring any additional memory to the fore. We even showed him pictures that he himself had taken, and no new memories were stimulated.

What are our conclusions? This study occupied our attention for approximately ten years. One of the things that we have underlined is the possibility of a research methodology which has proven to be fruitful. Frequently in studies of autobiographical memory, the researcher lacks a means to determine the extent to which an informant's memories are accurate representations of the events she purports to describe. Where available, the use of historical data and analysis to corroborate autobiographical memory perhaps has possibilities for future memory research.

While the memories presented here are primarily derived from just one individual, they indicate that within the range of human memory it is possible to reliably and accurately recover past events and to amplify and extend the existing written record. Howard's memories, however, are not accurate with respect to exact dates or to whether "the water was warm or cold." In this respect Cornelius Ryan is probably right. Our findings suggest that if it is details of this sort that are needed, oral history and oral interviews are probably not the best source. Howard only remembers the weather in connection with the bitter cold during the Bulge, but nowhere else does he mention it.

One element we found in these memories is that they are so stable, they are reliable to the point of being set in concrete. They cannot be disturbed or dislodged. It was virtually impossible to change, to enhance, or to stimulate new memories by any method that we could devise. We think, therefore, that we have a subset of memory, here called autobiographical memory, which is so permanent and so largely immutable that it is best described as *archival*. Now, it might be possible to find cues to elicit other memories, but the organization schema of archival memory seems to be such that unless you know exactly what those additional memories are, it is very, very difficult to find the appropriate cues. In the second recall document, for example, I knew what those cues were. I could say "rabbit" because I already knew what the schema was from the first interview. But lacking that knowledge, I had no way of using cues. So, as Marcel Proust has said in his great literary study of memory, "The past is hidden . . . beyond the reach of intellect, often in some material object. . . . And as for that object, it depends on chance whether we come upon it or not."[10]

Archival memory, as we conceptualize it, consists of recollections that are rehearsed, readily available for recall, and selected for preservation over the lifetime of an individual. They are memories which have been selected much as one makes a scrapbook of photographs, pasting in some and discarding others. They are memories which define the self and constitute the persona which one retains, the sense of identity over time. They enable us to see ourselves in the image of a sturdy youth, even though nobody, not even him, recognizes a picture of that youth when presented with it.

It appears that the impressions which are stored in archival memory are assessed at the time they occur, or shortly thereafter, as salient and hence important to remember. For this reason they are likely to be rehearsed or otherwise consolidated and become a part of archival memory. These events are thus likely to be unique happenings, or they are recorded because they are the *first* occasion upon which an event, which subsequently becomes more routine, occurred. Even occurrences which threaten the very life of an individual may be oldest in the stream of events if such an experience becomes sufficiently repetitive and routine. For example, Howard remembers firing the mortars only three times. He, of course, fired the mortars many hundreds, if not thousands, of times. We think that if for one reason or another an event is deemed sufficiently salient to a person's life, it *will* be rehearsed either internally or in conversation. It is commonplace in the language we use with these stories that, when they are rehearsed out loud, they are often concluded with the words, "I shall never forget it as long as I live." Our experiment verifies such a statement, if not for "as long as I live," then at least for forty years or more. We think that if this rehearsal fails to occur, however, the event will be unavailable by any ordinary means devised to bring it to the fore.

I think these findings share a number of implications for oral historians. One of the issues which has been debated at length is, How much preparation and detail about the issues under discussion is enough to conduct usual interviews? The conventional wisdom is that one can never feel they have done enough in this regard. Saul Bennison, author of the oral biography of Dr. Tom Rivers, has been the most dedicated and able advocate of the notion that intensely careful and detailed historical research is required prior to beginning an effective interview. I must confess that I had felt that he must be correct and had always crammed prior to doing an interview, saying to anyone, "Don't touch me, a fact will fall off." But this series of interviews with Howard indicates that intensive research designed to provide recognition factors has yielded minimal results. At the 1976 Oral History Association Colloquium an uncommonly provocative Canadian journalist, Barry Broadfoot, asserted that everyone has two well-rehearsed stories to tell, and when you've got them, you've got them. Pack your bags, leave, that's the end. His statement offended many more careful practitioners of the art of oral interviewing, but he may have made an important observation. It is true that most people have their memories for events stored under a number of very specific categories, chained to very specific associations. If that is true, it will be in fact a chancy business to attempt to find these categories in order to cue the memory. However, this picture need not be altogether discouraging for the efforts of oral interviewers to be rewarded. One of the major categories of organization seems to be chronological. Thus, taking a person in a time sequence through the events in which you are interested may lead to considerably richer memories for those events.

Benis Frank is the oral historian at the History and Museum Collection of the United States Marine Corps. He has interviewed hundreds of veterans of the United States Marine Corps, and when we started this project we asked his advice. He said, "Begin with Howard first entering the army. It will improve the interview." Certainly, when Howard was forced out of chronological sequence, he found it difficult to provide any narrative at all and created a recall document with significant deletions that he was able to reintegrate only after the first recall document was used to cue him. Therefore, preparation to engage an informant's attention, to make him or her feel that you are an informed listener, worthy of their honest and energetic effort, may well be adequate. It is relevant here to observe that Howard's conversations with his buddies at the reunion—men who had been where he had been, experienced what he had experienced—did not elicit more from Howard's memory than had been derived from the simple and straightforward request, "Tell me about the war and begin at the beginning."

II.

Howard S. Hoffman is an experimental psychologist and professor at Bryn Mawr College who has specialized in the scientific analysis of behavior, and in particular the mechanisms of learning and retention. In his early years in psychology, his research included a project to determine how long a carrier pigeon retained learned material. Hoffman was unable to find any evidence that the pigeon forgot as a function of elapsed time, but he recognized that emotional state was a factor in the learning process. This led him to research the startle mechanism as an indication of emotionality. In addition to his study of animal behavior, Hoffman has combined his personal talents and interests in art and in psychology to produce Vision and the Art of Drawing *(1989), which explains a technique he has developed to teach the art of drawing based on his research in sensation and perception. In this paper he expands the story of his recollective abilities, which he explored with his wife Alice Hoffman in* Archives of Memory: A Soldier Recalls World War II *(1991).*

When Alice and I started this project I had mixed feelings. As a scientist I was interested in learning something about the nature of long-term, autobiographical memory. As the subject, however, though I was curious about the possible results, I was also apprehensive. I knew I was going to dig into my memory claim on two widely separated occasions. I wondered if I would be consistent; that is, reliable in my recall. Would the stories change in their retelling, and if so how? Would there be a false progression toward making myself something of a hero? It also seemed possible that I might exhibit a loss of memories in the interval between recalls. After all, in my graduate work I had learned that we are born with a full complement of brain cells and that every day thereafter thousands of them die, never to be replaced. Would this be the fate of my memories? I was also concerned as to how I might react when I would eventually read the daily log from Company C, Third Chemical Mortar Battalion—my company. I had a dread of that log, that it might reveal some horrible event in which I had participated or witnessed but which I was unable to recall. I was also concerned that I might discover that I had fabricated or plagiarized some of what I believed to be my memories. I did not think this was likely, but I realized that the daily log might very well contain evidence pointing to this possibility. As near as we could tell, none of these nasty things happened. My memory claims turned out to be quite reliable.

Though not word-for-word identical, the stories I told during the second interview were very nearly the same as the ones I told during the first interview. What is equally important, there was not a story in the first document that was not also in the second document. If the amount of memory is determined by the number of brain cells, which I doubt that it is, then the inevitable loss of brain cells with aging is not a critical factor. My memory claims turned out to be largely valid, at least insofar as it was possible to check their validity by comparing them to the written record and to other available historical resources. This, too, need not have been the case. It was possible that my memory claims could have been perfectly reliable, could have related the same stories on both occasions, but these stories might have borne little resemblance to what was in the daily log of my company.

Elizabeth Loftus has shown us that eyewitness accounts are subject to considerable distortion by factors that occur after the events they describe. Alice has alluded to several examples of such distortions in my memory claims. One example was my failure to process and retain the return of the lost patrol in the fighting near Briançon. Another example was my failure to recall that the firing at Castleforte began at eleven p.m., not eleven a.m. as I suggested. A third example was my initial allusion to striped uniforms on the victims at Gardelegen. What seems surprising to me about these distortions is not that they occurred, but that there were so few of them.

Perhaps this means that the recollections that survive in archival memory are so well rehearsed that they are less susceptible to distortion than the more recent memories that Elizabeth Loftus has studied. Further research, however, would be needed before it could be determined if this is in fact the case.

More than twenty years ago, Alice's observations doing oral histories led me to hypothesize that certain memories can be so resistant to deterioration with time that they are best described as archival. I think that our study provides considerable support for this proposition. Marigold Linton's self-study of her memory of real-world events is relevant here. On the basis of her study, she was able to draw the following conclusions. Events are likely to endure in memory if they have these features: (1) they are perceived as highly emotional at the time they occur; (2) the subsequent course of events make the event appear to be instrumental or perceived as a turning point; and (3) the event must be relatively unique, not blurred by repetition.[11] Our study serves to confirm that these elements are also important in the formation of archival memories. This seems especially interesting in view of the differences between Linton's procedures and our own. In Linton's study, the events to be remembered were recorded by the subject, Linton herself, shortly after they occurred. Moreover, they were recorded in the context of the study of memory, a factor that could have affected what was selected and what would survive. In our study, the subject kept no diary and at the time of the events was not engaged in a study of memory. That these two studies should yield such similar conclusions despite these major differences serves to underline the importance of the factors they uncovered.

Alice discussed my inability to remember towing a target to sea during our preparations for the invasion of southern France. We now know that this event occurred; we have a photograph of it. Moreover, judging from my expression in the photograph, it seems obvious that this was an essentially pleasant experience for me. I can also state that at the time the photograph was taken, I was especially interested in the amphibious vehicle I was riding in. I know that this is the case because I had previously seen several such vehicles during the Battle for Rome, and I remember being very interested in them. For example, I remember noticing that these vehicles—they are called *ducks*—have propellers as well as wheels. And I wondered if the propeller was somehow geared to the wheels; that is, I wondered if the wheels would continue to revolve once the craft was in the water. I am certain that I must have learned the answer to this question when I helped to tow the target to sea, but I now have no idea of that answer. Nor do I know if we pulled the target to sea or pushed it. I don't even know if the target had an anchor, and if it did, whether it was fastened by a rope or a chain. In short, I remember nothing of the experience even though I have now examined the photograph hundreds of times. As Alice has suggested, we think that my subsequent preoccupation with the forthcoming invasion of southern France and/or my emotional reaction to the subsequent flash fire on the beach probably prevented the rehearsal that seems necessary for an experience to survive in archival memory.

There are those, however, who will argue that rehearsal has nothing to do with what is stored in memory and that the memory is there, but I just cannot get to it. I know that this is so because I have discussed the target-towing incident with many people, and there is always someone who has suggested that given enough psychoanalysis, or perhaps hypnosis, I might very well be able to recover this lost episode. I think that this suggestion is based on a tacit assumption that all experience is somehow permanently stored in memory. In this regard I can point out that while there is no way to prove that this is not the case, there are several observations that do argue against it. Perhaps the most cogent of these is that it would be extraordinarily inefficient for the brain to form a permanent record of every sight, sound, touch, taste, odor, pain, thought, and dream that occurs in the course of a lifetime. There are simply too many of them. Besides, we all know that some memories, such as those of certain telephone numbers, can be irretrievably lost within minutes—if not seconds—once we have dialed the number. Why would this happen if a record of every experience was always permanently stored in memory?

I think that our findings are consistent with the prevailing view that there are several kinds of memory, and that some of them require considerable rehearsal. As I have just suggested, one kind is short-term and disappears when it no longer needs to be retained. Other kinds of memory are semantic, or procedural, exemplified by the memories of how to read, how to ride a bicycle, or how to drive a car. These ordinarily require much rehearsal or practice, but once learned they exhibit little or no loss in memory over the course of a lifetime. Some experiences seem to leave lingering records. Endel Tulving calls them *episodic memories*. How long they are retained depends in part on how much we rehearse them. We remember what we had for breakfast today, or even dinner yesterday, though we may not have thought about it until now. But unless we actually rehearse these memories, it is doubtful we will be able to retain them for years, let alone decades, as seems to be the case with archival memories. When viewed from this perspective, archival memories are a subset of episodic memories. They consist of those special memories which, because of their relevance to our conception of ourselves, have been reviewed and pondered to the point that they have become indelible.

Notes

1. Thucydides, *The History of the Peloponnesian Wars*, ed. in translation by R. W Livingstone (Oxford: Oxford University Press, 1943), 40-41.

2. *The Second National Colloquium on Oral History at Arden House, Harrima New York, November 18-21, 1967* (New York: Oral History Association, 1968), 1 14.

3. Ibid.

4. John Mullen, interview with Alice Hoffman, February 1966, Pennsylvania Sta University United Steel Workers of America Archives, University Park, Pennsylvani 8-10.

5. Robert R. R. Brooks, *As Steel Goes, . . . Unionism in a Basic Industry* (Ne Haven: Yale University Press, 1940), 9.

6. John A. Neuenschwander, "Remembrance of Things Past: Oral Historians an Long-Term Memory," *Oral History Review* 6 (1978): 53.

7. W. G. F. Jackson, *The Battle for Rome* (New York: Scribner, 1969), 122-23.

8. "History of Company C, 3rd Chemical Battalion," Records of the Adjutan General's Office, 1917— , Entry 427 W.W. II Operations Report, 1940-48, Nationa Archives, Suitland, Md.

9. Conversation between Ralph Worley and Howard Hoffman, taped by Alic Hoffman, 21 September 1985.

10. Marcel Proust, *Remembrance of Things Past: Swann's Way* (New York Random House, 1934), 34.

11. Marigold Linton, "Real-World Memory after Six Years: An In Vivo Study o Very Long-Term Memory," in *Practical Aspects of Memory*, ed. M. M. Gruneberg P. E. Morris, and R. N. Sykes (London: Academic Press, 1978), 69-76.

COMMENT

Terry Anderson *is a professor of history and oral historian at Texas A&M University whose research interest centers on oral history research on the Vietnam war era in the United States, including both the homefront and war experiences.*

The Hoffman study raises a few important issues which concern historians. To oral historians the issue is memory, in this case the memory of Howard concerning his role in World War II. To all other historians the ssue is accuracy. Both written and oral historical documentation had iscrepancies; both were flawed, which is a painful lesson for historians.

The Hoffman study raises other questions about our discipline. What vas fact? What was fantasy? Their research demonstrates that memory is elective and dependent on individual experience. This was vividly lemonstrated in one of the most revealing episodes in their study, the mphibious vehicle incident. Howard not only could not remember the ncident, he had repressed it for some unknown reason. Even after seeing iimself in the picture he still was uncertain, until a ring on his finger and his comrades' explanations convinced him that he was there. Fact, not antasy. To mention a personal example, I visited Saigon last October, and is an historian of the Vietnam War, I had read much about the city and nterviewed many Vietnam veterans who had given me various impressions of the place. Their descriptions ranged from "Saigon was a lovely old French colonial capital" to "Saigon was a poor, dirty, decadent Babylon." Naturally, parts of the city in the 1960s and 1980s were both, but mportant here is that each person's memory of Saigon is colored more by experience than by the reality of the city.

Howard Hoffman's amphibious vehicle incident introduces another question: if the subject cannot remember the event, was it important enough to remember? I agree with Howard's comments: how inefficient for the brain to form a permanent record of every sight, sound, touch, taste, order. In interviews with over forty former students of Texas A&M University who became general officers and in interviews with dozens of Vietnam veterans, I have found a common theme which the Hoffman interviews bear out: each person fights his own war. What one soldier might remember is important to him because it was *his* memory—because he is unique—but it is not necessarily important to another who witnessed the event at the same place, same time. Perhaps a suggestion for the Hoffmans' research, then, is to conduct in-depth psychological interviews with Howard *and* with his brothers-in-arms, to try to ascertain why one soldier does and another does not remember certain details. Admittedly, this is a large order, but it could produce fascinating results for both psychologists and oral historians.

A related issue, and one that in my research I have found in common with the Hoffman study is this: what has been conducted by Alice Hoffman is an oral biography of a man at war, not a history of the war. Howard's remembrances are interesting to those who know him and possibly to those who served with him but are not of special importance to military historians of World War II. As Alice notes, Howard was not accurate with respect to the exact position of the army. The narrowness of personal meaning is a common encounter in interviews with veterans. A Vietnam veteran will tell me, "I just can't watch or read anything about

Vietnam since they tell of massacres or show American soldiers burnir
down Vietnamese homes. We never did that." True, that soldier, that pl
toon, during his one year in the country didn't burn homes or massac
civilians, but that does not mean that the other two and one-half millic
Americans during ten years of fighting didn't commit atrocities. After a
the My Lai massacre is fact. What we have is 2.5 million oral biographi
of World War II. The question for historians is: Which ones are importa
enough to be included in a general history of the war? It would be inte
esting, then, to conduct this type of research with General Eisenhower
General Westmoreland.

The Hoffman study also tells us about the job of oral historians. Barr
Broadfoot and Cornelius Ryan say that every individual has a few goo
stories or has memorized a few events from their past. Alice demonstrate
that there might be more. When she introduced the name of Howard'
captain, John Moore, Howard produced a recollection from "memory'
storehouse." As Alice notes, "Now Captain Moore was brought back t
what might be described as his rightful place in Howard's memory." Ou
job as oral historians is to find those Captain Moores, to do the back
ground research so we can elicit more from memory's storehouse.

Howard, in his comments, is surprised not that there were distortions i
his memory but that there were not more. I, too, am surprised. I hav
interviewed general officers in command positions who made numerou
factual errors. One general who served in World War II, Korea, an
Vietnam told me of an episode supposedly set in Korea. I sensed somethin
incorrect and questioned him. He looked perplexed and then said, "Oh
that might have happened in another war." What this suggests is that th
Hoffman study is significant for Howard Hoffman, but is it significant fo
others? How can it be generalized? Howard obviously has a super
memory; he also had an unimportant role in the war. What about a ma
with a poor memory who played a very important role? How would we ge
the most effective interview? Alice makes an important suggestion: whe
in doubt, conduct the interview chronologically. But does this study
suggest other hints?

Finally, this study demonstrates the potential for myth making in his
tory. What was real? What was unreal? There were minor discrepancie
concerning an enlisted man forty years ago in the Second World War, bu
what if they concerned the founding fathers two hundred years ag
recalling the making of the U.S. Constitution? How much of the history w
all are taught is myth? This study reminds us that history, including ora
history, is not a science but remains an art.

COMMENT

rent Slife *is a professor of psychology at Baylor University. He is a clinical sychologist who has conducted extensive research on metamemory.*

I would like to note the significance and globalness of the issues raised y the Hoffmans' presentations. Certainly their conclusions have a number f practical implications, including ramifications for my own discipline of linical psychology.

Let me begin, however, with a somewhat impractical observation. In er paper, Alice Hoffman asked how historians can know that informants' iemories are accurate representations of the events they purport to de-cribe. This question has been posed for centuries under many guises. imilar questions have been fundamental to epistemology and philosophy f science, to name just a few. In the epistemology of the seventeenth entury, John Locke postulated that our ideas, or memories, come from our xperience, which is itself founded upon the objects we sense in the xternal world. However, Locke left open the question that the Hoffmans ave raised: How well do these ideas correspond to the objects and events f reality? How can we ever be sure that our memories and ideas of reality ave ever been or ever will be representative of reality as it objectively is? Ve cannot escape the fact that we selectively attend to and structure eality, so how can we ever know how well, if at all, we have described it?

Some years after Locke, Bishop Berkeley offered a rather provocative olution that may have relevance for our discussion of this issue. He sserted that there is no permanent, material reality apart from our per-eptions.[1] All of these issues regarding accuracy of representation stem rom our assumption that there is an objective reality and that we should, herefore, find ways to objectively describe it. Berkeley would ask us to onsider instead the possibility that objective description is itself impossi-le and often simply not useful or meaningful, so why should we con-tantly strive for such goals?

This issue had been a hot topic in philosophy of science. Traditionally, cience has been viewed as a collection of objective facts. Indeed, cientists have striven to remove the human element from their fact athering. Newton, for example, advocated that scientists should not even nake hypotheses regarding their results because this ran the risk of biasing heir interpretation of the findings. Recently, however, many observers of cience, and scientists themselves, have given up on eliminating the human element in scientific theorizing and knowledge. They claim, much li Berkeley, that this is impossible and often not even desirable. So-call facts have never been objective; they are instead intersubjectively agre upon interpretations of the data. Newton's so-called Law of Gravity w not a fact but an interpretation of his data, later to be completely su planted by Einstein's explanations. Likewise, data by themselves a meaningless without human interpretation. That is, the human elements- interpretations, cognitive structurings and meanings that are given events—are absolutely essential to the knowledge of any thing or a event. We should not be attempting to study their influences and to u them appropriately in understanding our world.

If these trends in epistemology and philosophy of science can be giv any credence, they have interesting implications for our discussion her First, what does an historian like Cornelius Ryan, in the excerpt that Ali read, mean by "total accuracy"? Is this accuracy with respect to t events as they really happened? If so, what does "really happene mean? Or is this accuracy with respect to other subjective interpretatio of the events? If so, then Alice's point about the subjectivity of eve written documents shows that no historical source is necessarily closer what really happened than any other. Each has its own biased slant c reality, and our history in this sense can be likened to the facts of rece science; namely, intersubjective agreement of interpretation, with th possibility of replacement by another intersubjective agreement down th line—and not what "actually" happened, apart from the perception c humans.

This position by no means rules out investigations like the Hoffmans scientific investigation continues despite these developments i philosophy of science. In fact, a careful listener to their definitions c reliability and validity would note that they do not assume tradition objectivity. Reliability is the *consistency* of subjective impressions an memories, whereas validity is the *conformity between reports* of th events—not the conformity between reports and the event itself. In thi sense, the Hoffmans' research transcends these age-old issues. Remarkab intersubjective agreement was found, both across time (in the sense c reliability) and across sources (in the sense of validity). However, I woul caution us to temper our exuberance at these findings somewhat. There a many types of reliability and validity, and many questions about reliabilit and validity remain unanswered. For instance, to what extent can w generalize their data on reliability? Alice tells us that Howard avoide situations that might have influenced his memories of his war experienc How many oral informants will be doing this? What if they did not avoi related situations and experiences? Would their reliability as witnesses b ffected? I believe some of the findings by Elizabeth Loftus might indicate ss reliability, given relevant interceding experiences.

Another issue related to the validity of the Hoffmans' investigation is e fact that Howard is uncommonly sophisticated at observation and rec-llection. As an experimental psychologist he has done more than a little inking about memory processes generally and his own memory pro-esses specifically. It is true that he was not an experimental psychologist uring his wartime experiences, but his interest in and facility with memory rocesses might have preceded his ultimate vocation. In this sense, oward is not a representative informant, and the relatively high validity f his remembrances is probably not representative either. His memory ophistication is especially evident in this metamemory, or his ability to now what he remembers and know what he is less sure about remember-g. That is, Howard not only remembers the events of the past, he also elivers a running assessment of how well he remembers certain events ver others. I conduct research on metamemory, and I can tell you that eople differ greatly in this ability. A lack of metamemory can indeed affect e accuracy of the memories themselves. The point is that although the offmans' investigation is very well done and quite significant in my pinion, more work needs to be done before we can know just how reli-ble and valid their findings are with respect to other oral informants.

The emotional tone of our memories is to some extent in the eye of the eholder. As Alice noted, we have a mind's eye. Perhaps we cannot affect he particular memories that persist in our minds, but I would contend that ve can affect the impact or meaning of such memories. One of the poten-ially beneficial aspects of psychotherapy in this sense is that it can help he owner of the mind's eye adjust his or her beholding, or view, of the nemory. This would ultimately permit the meaning of the memory to be hanged so that is was less dysfunctional or less immobilizing. Of course, a hange in the meaning of the memory would also affect the interpretation f the event being remembered and brings us back to the epistemological ssue with which I began my commentary. Luckily, the Hoffmans' fine esearch is relatively free of such epistemological entanglements; however, broader discussion of these issues cannot avoid them.

Notes

1. See, for example, Thomas Leahey, *A History of Psychology: Main Currents in sychological Thought,* 2d ed. (Englewood Cliffs, N.J.: Prentice-Hall, 1987), 109.

DIALOGUE II

The following discussion among Donald A. Ritchie, Marigold Linton, Karen E. Fields, Alice M. Hoffman, Howard S. Hoffman, and Paul Thompson is based on the preceding essays.

DONALD A. RITCHIE: From time to time the Oral History Association has invited psychiatrists and psychologists to attend meetings to discuss memory and history issues, and somehow the dialogue hasn't always worked. I had a personal experience in that area at the second meeting I attended. I was interested in the phenomenon of exceptional memory and was working on two very lengthy interviews that were done by other people. When I interviewed mutual friends of the subjects, everyone seemed to mention that these people had photographic memories. I attended an Oral History Association meeting and went to a session in which a psychiatrist spoke on memory. During the coffee break, I stopped him and asked him what he thought about the concept of a photographic memory. He gave me an exasperated look and said, "There's no such thing," and rather abruptly turned and walked away and left me. Now, this might be one of those negative feelings that you would suppress in your memory except that the newsletter editor happened to snap a picture of this event. When I got my next issue of the Oral History Association newsletter, lo and behold, there was a photograph of the psychiatrist and me engaging in what seemed to be a very close and interesting discussion. This discussion lasted about three seconds, as I recall, and I would probably have forgotten the incident completely except for that photograph, which I see from time to time as I go back through old issues of the newsletter. In terms of documentation, that snapshot might be taken as an event that actually took place, something that I should remember and something that documented a major instance. In fact, the snapshot is much more misleading than the collage of my memory of that particular event. By contrast, the dialogue between historians and psychiatrists has really worked here.

MARIGOLD LINTON: Psychologists and oral historians both have special researcher-subject relationships, but we also represent a number of different kinds of relationships between researchers and their subjects. In my research, for example, I am *it*, that is, both subject and researcher—and you would think that this would make life simpler. I think that is not necessarily the case; it often makes it enormously difficult. You always wish

you had somebody else who could go back and look for the evidence
give an impartial point of view or do other sorts of things. The subje
usually arrives when you tell her to arrive, but not always even that!

ALICE M. HOFFMAN: As far as the relationship, in Marigold Linton
case it is her relationship with herself. In Karen Fields's case, it's h
relationship with her grandmother, and Howard and I are a married coupl
It certainly complicated it. The thing that blew me away about Kare
Fields's talk was that she made her relationship with her subject a positi
advantage, in that she took the dialogue between herself and her gran
mother and used it as an opportunity to instruct herself about the meanir
of the experience, so that her grandmother was certainly much more tha
simply an anthropological informant. That intrigued me because I have als
often felt that I learned a great deal from the interaction between myse
and the steelworkers that I was interviewing. What problems Howard an
I had, in terms of putting this together, happened when we tried to write
down. Then we had some really very serious altercations about how
should be said.

As far as further research is concerned, one of the things that intereste
me was that Howard, it seems to me, is unusually singly directed in terms
being a visual rememberer. Most people—I suspect but have no evidenc
for this, but I would like to see some more research on it—employ bot
visual and verbal strategies more usually. I think that it would b
interesting to see, in terms of interviewing in some depth about their ow
memory, someone who employs verbal strategies or a heavier mix
strategies. It would be interesting to see how that might affect the recogni
tion of items, because one of the things that is upsetting to me, as an or
historian, about our results is that all our hard work really did not produc
much more out of memory. The question then is, Is that because of th
nature of archival memory, or is it more likely to be a part of the particula
strategy that this rememberer utilized? I think we have to do more researc
before we have any hints as to which that might be.

HOWARD S. HOFFMAN: Among the researchers who were inter
viewing either themselves, a grandmother, or a husband, there seemed t
be a more positive approach or at least a feeling about the information tha
was gathered from it. Among the researchers who did not know thei
subjects so well, a little more professional and scholarly skepticism wa
applied to the value of much of the interview material. Paul, since yo
raised in your initial remarks some skeptical approaches to the value
interviewing, I wondered about your observations on that.

PAUL THOMPSON: I would not say that what I was trying to put for
ward was a skeptical view of the value of interviewing. It was, on th
contrary, meant to suggest that even if you are skeptical of the absolut
truth or not of what you hear, that there is a great deal that you can mak
of it, and that what people say when it is in sort of absolute terms "no

rue” is as interesting as what they say when it is true. I think there is a great deal more work to be done if we are to get any really valuable junction between the kind of psychology we have been hearing and the kind of work that we do in oral history. I think that there are some reasons which are fairly easy to tackle. One is simply that what psychologists call long-term memory turns out to be usually a matter of a year at the very most, a couple of years perhaps, and oral historians are dealing in much longer memory. So very few of these experiments really have much direct relevance to what we are doing.

There is a more fundamental problem, and that is the sort of conceptual assumptions, the unspoken assumptions, in all the psychology papers which are still positivistic, where oral history was twenty years ago, even ten years ago. In oral history we have moved very rapidly from that position, and I don’t see that kind of movement going on in what we have heard from psychology. I think it would be possible to introduce more of the understanding that we have gained into psychological work. I noticed, for instance, this idea that the archival memory is somehow a fixed one. Now, that is so like what Jan Vansina was saying in the 1960s, but that is a view that has now really been rejected as quite untenable. I find it disturbing, that kind of concept as the way of working with the material. I think we need something actually different.

I have been thinking about Marigold Linton’s point that a person’s memory was going to be less when it referred to negative experiences than to positive ones. It seems to me that, there again, behind that is the assumption there is something rather fixed called memory and that that is all that we are dealing with. Actually, I think that there are other, quite different factors involved which explain that. From my experience in interviewing—and it is quite true that there is a tendency to put a positive interpretation on experience—but that is not the whole of what is going on. Very often you find strange and fascinating discordances between the overall interpretation and the actual information that people give you. I think that that is, in a way, more what we should be trying to look at. I mean, not being absolute, quantified, balanced between positive and negative memory, but actually looking for reasons why there are those differences and what explains them.

If I could just give you an example of the way I am thinking: Just over the last few weeks I have been looking at a set of about fifty interviews in which people are talking about their married lives. One of the things that really struck me very powerfully was that the interviews describe rather a similar sort of balance of patterns, such as the way people evaluate their marriages in terms of, say, role division, so that if I came in with my subjective judgment and started saying, Well, I think this is a rather close marriage, and that is a very role-divided one, and so on, the proportions would balance out. Yet, when you turn to the interviewees’ own evalua-

tions in the actual language they use to describe their marriages, there is a
extraordinary difference between people who are still married and peopl
who are widowed. So it is the *interpretation* that has changed. And tha
is, of course, not because something has happened to their memories, bu
because they are at different points in their life experiences, and so th
interpretation is changed. Again, I would want to suggest on this poin
that *forgiveness* is a very important factor. As people get older, they ma
not change their absolute memories of unpleasant things from the past, bu
sometimes they are able to reach forgiveness, which changes the whol
quality of memory. So what I am saying is that I am not satisfied by a ver
positivistic, scientific approach in the narrow sense. I would like to see
movement from the psychologists, a recognition of the broader and mor
humanistic qualities in oral history work.

H. HOFFMAN: You have thrown down the gauntlet. I wonder what evi
dence you have to discount the idea of archival memory. I thought w
were presenting scientific data that was open to whatever interpretatio
you want. In the documents that we presented, there is no evidence of
loss of memory there. There was no evidence of loss of memory with th
passage of time. You said that there was evidence against the idea and tha
it had been discounted. What was the evidence?

THOMPSON: I did not say that there was evidence against the notion o
archival memory. What I said was that that notion had very close parallel
with the approach that Jan Vansina had to oral tradition in the 1960s, the
idea that there was a collective memory which could be passed down in
unchanged nuggets. I think that what is now understood much more
clearly is the way that collective memory is continually molded and re-
molded by a whole series of different influences. I would argue that the
exact same thing happens with individual memory.

A. HOFFMAN: I think that one of the contributions that psychologists
have to make to oral historians is their very strong grounding in data. Now,
there can be lots of different efforts to interpret data in terms of what it
means. But if you do a study like Marigold Linton has done, or if you do a
study like Elizabeth Loftus has done—providing the study is not flawed
methodologically—it presents you with what then becomes certain facts.
You can disagree about what these facts mean, but what you cannot
disagree about is the fact that there is something there. When Marigold
talks about, for instance, the Pollyanna Principle, she is describing an effect
that has been demonstrated over and over again by psychologists; that is,
people simply remember more good stuff than they do bad stuff at
whatever period in their lives that you interview them. It is a very robust
effect. Now, we can argue about why that is. For instance, if you wanted
to have the most optimistic view of the world possible, you could say
people have more good experiences than bad experiences. Or you could
say, No, there is a higher degree of forgetting of bad experiences. Or you

could say, as Paul is saying, that there is a life-course effect here, and it depends upon when you dip into it where you see this effect most profoundly. But what you can't argue about is that there is such an effect. Folks simply do remember more good things than they do bad things.

THOMPSON: I think you've made your argument very strongly, but I just think that you cannot make absolute assertions. I mean, it really depends on what you are talking about. The idea that people have quantifiably more good memories than bad ones is one which—I mean, I wouldn't want to start thinking about memory as if it were a series of pennies, and you could say, We'll put a pile of bad pennies there and a pile of good pennies there. Anybody, for instance, who worked as a psychoanalyst would find it rather difficult to recognize the idea that people's memories on the whole were very good.

LINTON: It wouldn't take twenty-five years to complete analysis if it were easier to get at the negative memories! But let me just say in response to Alice's summary, where she said it could be because you have more positive events to remember, those of you who are interested in that subject really should read Matlin and Stang, who say something like this: You probably have more positive experiences. If you don't, you are probably leading your life wrong, because you determine what situations you expose yourself to. If it looks like it is going to be an ugly experience to come to Baylor, for example, you stay home. You tend to expose yourself to more positive experiences. You will avert your gaze from that statue in Charleston, or go poke holes in it, or whatever. But every step along the way, people tend to do that.

Was it Henry Higgins who said, "And why can't a woman be more like a man?" I think that at least part of the problem here is that I would like all of the oral historians to become psychologists. But just exactly what is exciting about people from different disciplines meeting is that we are all looking at the thing differently. I had said to a number of people privately after Paul's talk, "Oh, if only I could give a talk that was that elegant! If only I had that sweep." Psychologists are always dealing with grumpy little picky stuff. And then I said, "But of course! If I were an historian, would I be saying, Why am I wasting my time with history? Why aren't I a theologian so I could really get the broad sweep of where we are and where we're going?" I mean, we know that twenty years from now our disciplines are not going to look like they do now, and we are all fooling ourselves about how important our data are. There are always going to be other ways that are going to inform us more. I'm always embarrassed that psychology informs us as little as it does, and I do my best to inform as much as I can. But it only informs within a narrow framework, as history does.

H. HOFFMAN: I was thinking as we have discussed positives and negatives that it also depends on who is doing the interpreting of what is a positive and what is a negative. In Karen Fields's remarks about her grandmother's trip on the boat to New York, what to her grandmother was a positive trip, Karen was looking for a negative: segregation. But that was not how her grandmother valued that trip in any way. What I got out of Karen's remarks was that you have to sometimes turn your scholarly impressions upside down, to listen to what the informant has to say, and to take their memories on their own terms. There is sort of a sensitivity to the varieties of memory, I suppose, that we are addressing.

KAREN E. FIELDS: I am hesitant to say that I could identify, except in the most extreme cases, what a good or bad memory is for somebody else. I don't know how I would go about identifying from a stream of talk what was good or bad. I know that I am very good at concealing such in my own talk. It is part of negotiating reality, social reality in many instances, to retain as private what doesn't have to be the business of the interlocutor. If I had myself as a research subject, I would know better. But if I were working with another subject, I don't know how I would discover, with any certainty, when the Pollyanna Principle was at work. And if I hadn't been dealing with a subject like my grandmother, but had been dealing with the generally much more supine subjects you encounter when you sally forth from academe or when you sally from your professorial podium down to your students, I am not sure how much resistance comes to the interpretations or the coding that you do as a researcher to the sorting of events. "I went and bought a huge bag of groceries" is for me a negative experience because I hate shopping. But if I had arrived from a place where groceries were a luxury, I think the valuation would be different. That is a trivial example. I think we would all agree, when it came to life and death, sickness and health, that most of life isn't that simple. Then the rest of memory involves coloring and shading. I pick up on Paul's language of the good pennies and bad pennies; I would have a lot of trouble knowing how to sort for someone else.

A. HOFFMAN: To get at the issue about sorting the pennies into good pennies and bad pennies—and I would certainly like to be corrected by Marigold on this if I'm wrong, because I am not a psychologist—but the studies that I am familiar with indicate that sorting is a self-assessment. The person who is the subject is asked to say for themselves whether the experience was a good one or a bad one.

LINTON: Let me just describe one of these studies. A typical way a study would be run is this: Remember that psychologists usually deal with very short time spans. A kid comes back from summer vacation, and the teacher asks, "What did you do during the summer?" The kid writes down what she did during the summer. The teacher says, "How much fun did you have?" And the kid ranks the experiences. Then, six weeks later, six months later, a year later you say, "What did you do last summer?" And you find very simply that the recounting of the items includes mostly the positive; the kid won't include the items she ranked as negative.

This, incidentally, is typical enough that you find some very interesting behaviors that are based on it. For example, if you have people who are just getting a divorce and you say, Why are you doing this?, the answer starts with the negatives and they have a list of reasons. But as time goes by, the negative items fall out. You know how often people end up with reconciliations? You find people who are getting ready to get married again, and you can watch this incredible pull toward the positive memories. But often the negative information is reinstated very, very rapidly; they are right up there again at the top of the list, and then he/she leaves him/her at the altar. But as they move away from the experience, the negative cues drop out—Howard knows this from his work on animals—their aversion decreases. Psychologists can look at those things and you see them very nicely occurring again and again. Those memories are self-rated; they are self-imposed. The memory is very dependent on how close you are to the cues, and the further you are away in time, the lower the negative effect. You are left with the positive memories and you engage in some stupid behavior.

FIELDS: May I change the subject? I would like to ask how psychologists define memory. I am responding to what I hear, and I think that I must operate in a realm that is different somehow. I hear *memory* being used as something that can be assigned an "a," to "a memory." I am wondering to what extent, for purposes of research, memory becomes an object, something that is remembered. If it does, then what is the relationship of that object, some *thing* that is remembered, to something larger which one could call processes or faculties? We have a piece of vocabulary that doesn't have the same meaning to everybody. I tend to think of memory as a set of faculties, but I think I hear it understood in the operations of researchers—you all do it—as objects that are related in some way to faculties, meaning the capacity to do X number of operations of X kind that have to do with retrieval and positioning of information.

A. HOFFMAN: I think you make a very, very good point, Karen, because the new studies of memory—the cognitive studies of memory, of which Marigold's work is an example—have come along and said memory is not a unitary process. The earlier studies of memory looked at memory as though it were a thing, but the cognitive psychologists have come along and said no, there are *kinds* of memory. There are a variety of processes here. There is episodic memory, there is autobiographical memory, there is semantic memory, there is procedural memory—memory for how you go about the process of retrieving information. And there are all these different kinds of things, and they may actually have different rules and different locations in the brain. They may be quite different, one from the other. That new perspective of looking at memory is something that is generating a lot of research just now that is quite different from the old nonsense, the laboratory study in which you try to suck all the meaning away from the memory. The new memory theorists came along and said, Well, you are not studying memory. You are studying something that takes place in the laboratory, but you are not studying it in a naturalistic environment where it has any meaning at all. That is a new, exciting thing that is just starting to happen.

H. HOFFMAN: I would address it a little differently. Oral historians interview informants about events they have witnessed, and generally they witnessed or experienced them some distance in the past. One of the questions that one has to ask about the descriptions that the informant provides is, To what extent are those descriptions likely to be reliable? That was the question that we were asked. We did not know what we were going to find when we did the study. It could have turned out that I told one set of stories in 1978 and an entirely different set of stories in 1982, and that when I told the same story about the same thing, it wasn't the same. That was always a possibility. But there is some question about how reliable these memories are that we carry with us.

Life is really based on memory. There is an interesting little experiment you can do: We blink our eyes maybe fifteen or twenty times a minute. Every time we blink our eyes, the room goes dark. We don't notice this. The reason we don't notice this is because it has been shown that the brain preserves the image that you are looking at at the moment that the blink occurs, and that is what you are looking at during the blink. I can describe the experiments that will prove that to you, but an even simpler one that you can try for yourself is to take a mirror, hold it about six inches in front of your eyes, and look from one eye to the other. You will not be able to see your eyes move, although if you look at somebody else doing that or have somebody look at you doing it, it is very easy to see the eyes move. The reason that you don't see the eyes move is because when we make a movement of the eyes of this sort, the brain suppresses input and retains what you were looking at just before you moved your eyes. Now, what it means is that what we *perceive* in the world is what we *remember* of the world. We do not ever perceive the world as it is existing at a particular moment. It takes an insignificant amount of time for the light to stimulate the retina, but it does not take an insignificant amount of time for those biochemical reactions to cause the neurons in the optic nerve to fire and to pass through six or seven different sequences of neurons before they get back to the occipital part of the brain where we then perceive some visual experience. We do not have direct contact with the world about us and, in a very real sense, I think that the study of memory is really the study of how we are able to have continuity in a world that is constantly changing.

One of the commentators suggested that maybe I have a special kind of memory, and perhaps I do, although I don't think of myself this way. I would very much hope that this kind of study could be repeated so that we could have more than one in the study. Each of us carries with us some kinds of memories that we use to define ourselves, the corpus of our experience that we carry with us from day to day. We have not tested it; most of us don't test ourselves on it, and most of us probably never will. But for most people, if you think back to some memory that you have now, that you have carried for an extended period of time—ten to twenty years—it is very unlikely, from the data that we have, that four years from now it is going to change. When you find a phenomenon in even a single subject, what you are showing is what the possibilities are. You are showing something of the character of the phenomenon that you are studying. In our case what we have shown is that, at least for the present, it is a better bet that certain memories are relatively permanent than it is that they are going to change very much in the near future.

RITCHIE: Certainly the one thing that we all have in common is that in our professions we do interviewing, and in our interviewing we all encounter memories, and every memory, it appears, is somehow different.

AFTERWORD

LEARNING MEMORY AND REMEMBERING HISTORY

Lewis M. Barker

Lewis M. Barker is Professor of Psychology at Baylor University, where he teaches courses on neuroscience and learning and behavior.

Oral historians and psychologists alike are concerned with the origin and fate of memories. The task of both types of researchers is to determine *when* and under *what conditions* a memory is first acquired, *how* to ascertain whether the recalled memory is veridical, and if it is not, *why* not. What is the significance of *forgetting*? And under what conditions are memories *fabricated* or otherwise *reconstructed*?

Because the education and resulting research interests of historians and psychologists have them asking markedly different questions about the nature of memories, we should not be surprised when philosophical and methodological gaps between them occur. This volume is no exception. Each type of researcher brings *a prioris* and methodological assumptions to his or her study of memory. Psychologists in laboratories using human and animal subjects assume that the determinants of memory can be repeatedly manipulated and accurately measured. Oral historians "in the field" almost exclusively study human memories as they are recalled many years after being formed. Should we be surprised when each type of researcher occasionally misses the point of the other's enterprise?

A central question running throughout this volume is the extent to which common interests in human memory can overcome the different ways in which historians and psychologists are trained to study, and ultimately to understand, the human mind. Two recent books are relevant to this enterprise, and both are highly recommended. *Memory Observed: Remembering in Natural Contexts*, edited by Ulric Neisser, is an acknowledged classic in cognitive psychology. Neisser's selection of research articles reveals both the perils and promise of applying laboratory-derived models of memory and cognition to instances in real life. *Memory in the Real World* builds upon and updates the same themes. The present analysis takes advantage of ideas derived from both books.[1]

The present paper has three purposes: (1) to observe how historians and psychologists, respectively, study memory, with the hope of capturing the threads which tie together their endeavors; (2) to point out benefits and drawbacks associated with each discipline's methods and to suggest ways in which they may complement each other in future research; and (3) to analyze selected research findings in this volume from the perspective of findings in experimental psychology—specifically, from the study of perception, learning, and short-term memory.[2]

THE PROBLEM OF VERIDICAL MEMORY

For a memory to be veridical, it must accurately reflect the event being remembered. Given that no two individuals experience the world in the same way, questions about truthfulness of memory are also questions about the *perception* of reality. Stating the obvious, veridicality of memory is initially dependent upon "correct" perceptions.

One could naively argue, for example, that matching one's memory for an event with a videotape of the same event (the videotape of the event being the "real" percept) would be a way to assess veridicality of memory. However, such argument begs the question: Do two observers, be they subjects or experimenters, see the videotape in the same way? Likely not. Psychologists (psychophysicists, to be more precise) who study perceptual processes have measured how well the "real world" is mapped. And, with the exception of simple stimuli (pure tones, flashes of colored light, et cetera) human judgments have been shown to be easily biased by social factors.[3] These biased perceptions are subsequently encoded into memory.

MEMORY AS VIDEOTAPE

Considering further the example, let us show the videotape of an episode to a variety of individuals. We will ask them first to describe the scenario, and later to recall the events as depicted in the scenario. Is this a simple memory experiment? No, and for reasons other than the above-mentioned problem of individual biases in perception. Elizabeth Loftus and her colleagues have demonstrated that the memory of what is perceived can also be biased by the experimenter's verbal suggestions as to what is being viewed on the videotape—analogous to "leading the witness." In one of her studies, a subject views a videotape of two cars impacting. The experimenter asks ("suggests") whether the two cars "bumped" or "crashed" together. Which word is used apparently has the effect of reconstructing the subject's memory in one of two ways, consistent with the experimenter's language.

Humans are apparently "easily led" in what they perceive and in what they remember.

CULTURE BIASES PERCEPTION

For yet other reasons descriptions of memories using the videotape methodology is not as simple as it seems to be. Glenace Edwall reminds us that a person's culture also dictates one's perceptions; we have been conditioned to see and hear (and thereby remember) in highly constrained ways. The psychological deafness required of Japanese families who live in houses with paper walls is one example; a child's denial and resulting memories of an incestuous relationship *not* remembered as an adult is another.

RESEARCHERS' BIASED MEMORIES

Bias in perception leads to bias in memory. Accuracy of memories suffers from other factors as well. Historical and psychological theories, for example, delimit the ways in which verbalized memories are heard and interpreted by researchers. A recent criticism of Sigmund Freud's work, for example, is that he interpreted his female patients' reports of incest as sexual fantasies rather than as accurate memories. One interpretation of his deafness to the possibility of veridical reports from these women is that he assumed that his culture was civilized in such a way so as to preclude rampant sexual abuse of children by adult males. Our current knowledge that incest is prevalent in Western culture now allows researchers to "hear" their patients explore such memories.

Furthermore, how we educate our children will influence what they perceive and what they will remember as adults. Cultures acknowledging incest and other forms of abuse likely will produce children who will encode and report such events when they occur and will be more inclined to recall them in the future.

The problem of the perception of reality hampers not only subjects, then, but also flavors interpretations of reality by researchers. We design experiments with preconceived results in mind; is it any wonder when our interpretation of results reflects these biases? Perhaps the best we can do at present is try to understand the *zeitgeist* of both the researcher and of the individual (i.e., their biases), to recognize the cultural milieu at the time a given memory was formed, and only then make a best guess as to whether a reported memory is veridical.

SCIENCE AND HISTORY: METHODS AND GOALS

Another theoretical/methodological difference between historical accounts and scientific findings concerns the role of *evidence*. In science, causal relations are validated by a consensus of observers (cf., the necessity of both *inter-observer agreement* and the requirements of *replicability*). Oral historians do not experiment, precluding replicability of their observations. Achieving inter-observer agreement *is*, however, within their methodological realm. In theory, inter-observer agreement on historical evidence would help close the methodological gap with the behavioral sciences and their more stringent requirements of evidence.

Is it possible to achieve a consensus of agreement among scientists studying memory in laboratories and among historians interviewing subjects at different times and places in the field? Scientists have the luxury of repeating their memory experiments when they cannot agree upon the experimental outcome. For example, Scientist B might challenge an interpretation of Scientist A by copying Scientist A's experiment, changing one or more critical aspects of it, perhaps including a demonstration of the effect of another variable in an experimental replication. This widespread research tactic defines so-called "normal" science.

HISTORY AS BEHAVIORAL SCIENCE: A CASE STUDY

Can historians do "normal science"? Let us take as an example research reported in this volume by Michael Frisch. Over a period of many years he asked his students what they remembered about famous historical figures from American history. He used a variant of the *method of free recall*, commonly used in the laboratory by memory researchers. One important methodological difference is that psychologists typically control presentation and rehearsal of the items to be recalled, whereas Frisch measures end-point performance of school work learned (or not) over an extended time period.

Frisch correctly points out that he lost data in his research by collapsing across *order of item recalled*. Had he retained the order in which students remembered historical names (i.e., the first famous person which came to mind, then the second, et cetera) he more than likely would have found a serial position effect in the list of names recalled by his students.

Simply stated, the serial position effect describes a bow-shaped relationship between the frequency (number) of items recalled from a list when plotted as a function of the *order* of items on the list. First and last items appearing on the list are recalled with a higher frequency (i.e., remembered better) than items in the middle.

For ninety years the serial position effect has been the object of intensive study by psychologists because of what it tells us about how lists of tems are encoded into memory.[4] One might argue that only psychologists certainly not historians!) would be interested in a serial position effect and elated memory concepts of *primacy* (first items on the list are remembered better), *recency* (last items on the list are remembered better), and *anchoring* (position cues affect which items are remembered).

How can the order in which names are recalled be of value to the historian or to educators interested in teaching history? Frisch used the prompt "American history from its beginning through the end of the Civil War" to elicit the list of historical figures. This prompt provided two anchors ("beginning," and "Civil War," respectively) around which individual names were recalled. Even without the serial-order data, by inspecting the rank order of names we can make educated guesses about the order in which items were recalled. For example, we can surmise that the first name remembered was that of Washington and the second that of Lincoln—one for each anchor. Note in Table 1.4 that five names cluster around the first anchor (i.e., Washington, Jefferson, Franklin, Adams, and Revere around "beginning"), while three names cluster around the second anchor (Lincoln, Grant, and Lee around "end of Civil War"). One can speculate that Columbus's ranking of ninth on the list would improve had the anchor differed (i.e., had the prompt been "From the *discovery* of America" rather than "From the *beginning* of America").

As every teacher knows, questions must be carefully worded; many "wrong" answers reflect students' idiosyncratic but understandable misinterpretations of the question. The use of two anchors in the prompt has the effect of determining particular items and the order of their recall. Frisch's methodology is different than that used in Loftus's research, but the finding is the same. The experimenter's choice of words in the prompt suggests (cues) *what* is remembered. In the present instance, both an evaluation of student curriculum and of student performance hang critically upon the selection of words comprising the question.

Readers who remain skeptical about the relevance of the serial position effect for the recall of historical knowledge are directed to research by Henry Roediger and Robert G. Crowder.[5] They allowed college students five minutes to write the names of all American presidents they could remember "in any order." These psychologists found the now familiar serial position effect—first and last presidents were remembered better than the intermediate ones.

TIME EFFECTS IN HISTORY AND PSYCHOLOGY

In their memory research Paul Thompson and Karen Fields address th importance of *location* in *time*. Their subjects' memories were often tied t a house in which successive generations had lived. By contrast, scientist generally believe that their observations are "timeless," that is, ar repeatable *irrespective of time and place*. That "Science" produces find ings that can be replicated in laboratories around the world is a commonl held belief.

In fact, however, for many years behavioral scientists experimenting o how humans and animals learn and remember in the laboratory have bee aware of the importance of *context*. For example, rats and other ex perimental subjects *trained* to criterion in one apparatus have been show to respond differently when transferred and *tested* in another. Likewise students who hear lectures and take notes in one room will perform bette when tested *there* than if moved to another location. These so-called *con text*, or *state dependent* effects, are presumably due to the fact that memo ries of the environment (cf., context) are inextricably bound to and learne in conjunction with the target memories in question.

Should we be surprised, then, when a visit to an elementary school re leases a flood of memories? Even more importantly, the above laborator research predicts that the field researcher will get better memory reports (o at least, *different* memories) if the subject is interviewed where the memor was formed.

SHORT-TERM AND LONG-TERM MEMORY

Oral historians restrict their study of memory to what psychologists call "long-term memory." We noted in analyzing both Loftus's and Frisch's research that *recall* from long-term memory is heavily influenced by the nature of queries addressed to that memory. The *contents* of long-term memory are mostly (exclusively?) determined by *acquisition* processes which occur during the operation of "short-term memory."

Here we ask whether studies of short-term memory, that is, of the conditions under which memories are *acquired*, are relevant to issues governing recall of long-term memories, a domain of particular interest for oral historians and psychologists alike.

What better place to start than with the work of Alice and Howard Hoffman, who discuss the role of *emotion* in acquiring memories. Alice Hoffman (historian) and Howard Hoffman (experimental psychologist) discuss the finding that many incidents are apparently remembered with *less* emotion as time passes from the time of encoding—the so-called "Pollyanna effect." (I shall return to this point later.)

One possibility raised by the phenomenon of emotional decay of memory is that memories are not constant events but rather are dynamic in time—that the form and content of a memory is in part dependent upon *when*, after encoding, the memory is recalled. The Hoffmans followed up on this idea in their most recent work. They posit that after a critical amount of time has elapsed following the encoding of the target memory, *archival memories* are formed. Archival memory is so permanent and resistant to change that written records and other forms of evidence to the contrary are ineffective in "correcting" the nonveridical target memory.[6]

LEARNING LIFE'S MEMORIES

Can theory and research in experimental psychology shed light on the foregoing aspects of dynamic memory? One key may lie in an analysis of how life's memories are acquired in the first place. With all due respect to Carl Jung's notion of inherited memories (i.e., the *collective unconscious*), most if not all memories are *learned*. Psychologists specializing in the study of learning assume that many long-term memories are acquired as the result of learned associations between events.

For example, I have only two or three memories from my fourth year of life. Why do I retain these memories to the exclusion of others? In one I am lying on a table watching my right hand wave a small American flag. I presume that I remember this image in part because of the events surrounding this episode. My father has described to me (and I vaguely remember) how he gently held me down with an ether-soaked cloth over my nose and mouth while acting as an anesthesiologist for a country doctor who proceeded to remove my tonsils. My most vivid memory is of seeing the flag waving and of the smell of ether; later I remember the bitter taste of Aspergum brought by an uncle following the surgery, and how the taste of the gum affected the taste of ice cream I painfully (dutifully) swallowed.

Is it as obvious to the reader as it now is to me that the flag became a memory because it symbolized an overwhelmingly emotional occasion? The flag became associated with a small child's suffocating fear. Interestingly, I can't remember "seeing" any other details of the room—neither my father nor the doctor nor (according to family accounts) the uncle who was present during the incident.

The "taste of Aspergum"? Forever associated with a sore throat. Interestingly, I have a vague remembrance of my uncle who produced the gum from his pocket.

THE CONDITIONING OF MEMORIES

Ivan Pavlov was the first to demonstrate in a laboratory that a novel "neutral" stimulus (any stimulus producing a sensation—a bell, a small American flag, the taste of Aspergum) would be remembered better if it were associated with a "biologically meaningful stimulus." Pavlov rang a bell, then placed food in a dog's mouth, eliciting reflexive salivation. By ringing a bell and following it with food, Pavlov loaded into the dog's memory a special significance for "a ringing bell." Again, with no Jungian overtones intended, food already has a special significance for the dog due to genetic inheritance (cf., a "biologically meaningful" stimulus). In my case, the flag was associated with the "biologically meaningful" stimulus of foul-smelling ether and the fear-inducing gestalt of the surgery episode.

In 1920 John B. Watson similarly conditioned "Little Albert" by showing the eleven-month-old infant a white rat. Initially, Albert, a normally curious child, showed no fear as he reached out to touch and explore this "neutral" stimulus. Watson then waited for Albert to visually locate and reach for the rat. At an opportune time Watson struck a steel bar (suspended behind the child's head) with a hammer. From Watson's written account the loud and unexpected clanging sound gave the infant a horrible fright, causing him to cry. After seven such pairings of "rat" with "frightening noise," Watson presented the rat by itself. Not surprisingly, the child cried and tried to get away. A month later Albert's memory of the conditioning procedure persisted, and Watson mused that unless the memory was experimentally altered, it would persist into adulthood as a phobia.[7]

The point of recounting these memories of bells, flags, and rats is not to suggest that we remember only vividly aversive events but rather that in the welter of information bombarding us hourly, daily, and throughout a lifetime, some episodes *are* singled out and remembered better than others. Among this category of memories are episodes in which we were *emotionally* involved. These memories tag significant occasions in our lives.

THE EXTENSION OF EMOTIONAL COMPONENTS OF MEMORIES

To return to a question raised by the Hoffmans in this volume: Why a "Pollyanna effect" in which the aversiveness associated with a memory decreases over time? One interpretation is suggested by the research of Pavlov and others into how conditioned responses can be *extinguished*. Recall that after conditioning dogs to salivate, Pavlov rang the bell and did not present food. The conditioned response to the bell diminished, a phenomenon he called experimental extinction. Is it unreasonable to suggest that the dog initially experienced a psychological/emotional state not unlike that of "disappointment" in humans when the bell rang and food was withheld? Further, that the dog became less emotional as it relearned, with repeated extinction trials, that the food was no longer forthcoming?

Forty years after the fact, my "flag" memory is a relatively dispassionate one. I suspect that the many iterations of this memory during the days immediately following my tonsillectomy allowed extinction of the emotional arousal attendant with that memory. I am left with a scripted story, some fading visual images, and little memory of the degree of fear experienced during my fourth year.

Our meager understanding of human behavior profits both from the study of psychology and from the study of history. Of the two the latter seems to be the more complex endeavor. Oral histories are accounts of human behavior based upon memories that have been encoded through perceptual processes colored by the biases of culture, the vagaries of emotion, the distortions of time, and the lability of researchers blind to the *zeitgeist* within which they work. The conceptual tools and methods of experimental psychology do not and cannot inform all aspects of the study of history or, for that matter, of the study of human behavior. Indeed, experimental psychologists and historians alike continue to raise far more questions about human behavior than they provide answers, or even partial truths.

Most marriages have rocky starts; the present one is no exception. The articles collected in this volume bespeak the fertility and promises of an overdue union.

Notes

1. Ulric Neisser, ed., *Memory Observed: Remembering in Natural Contexts* (San Francisco: W. H. Freeman, 1982); Gillian Cohen, *Memory in the Real World* (London: Lawrence Earlbaum Associates, 1989). Neisser's edited book contains articles by Marigold Linton and Elizabeth Loftus, both of whom are contributors to this volume.
2. Learning and memory constructs developed by experimental psychologists can be differentiated from psychoanalytical constructs so popular with many historians. By and large Freud's theories, including that of unconscious motivation and the defense mechanisms of repressed memory, while not without merit, lack an empirical base.
3. Classic work by Solomon Asch demonstrated that even when making simple judgments, such as estimating the length of a line, a person's perception can be

influenced by peers making conflicting estimates. The evidence of raw sensory experience yields to the pressure to conform with the group's judgment. S. E. Asch, "Studies of independence and conformity: I. A minority of one against a unanimous majority," *Psychological Monographs* 70 (1952), Whole No. 416.

4. The serial position effect was first reported in 1902 by Hermann Ebbinghaus in *Grundzuge der Psychologie* (Leipzig: von Veit, 1902). An overview of the serial position effect can be found in Robert G. Crowder, *Principles of Learning and Memory* (Hilldale, N.J.: Lawrence Erlbaum Associates, 1976).

5. Henry L. Roediger III and Robert G. Crowder, "A Serial Position Effect in Recall of United States Presidents," in Neisser, *Memory Observed*, 230-37.

6. Alice M. Hoffman and Howard S. Hoffman, *Archives of Memory: A Soldier Recalls World War II.* (Lexington: The University Press of Kentucky, 1990).

7. John B. Watson and Rosalie Rayner, "Conditioned Emotional Reactions," *Journal of Experimental Analysis of Behavior* 3 (1920): 1-20.

321015